# SEIZE THE MOMENT, SHARE THE MESSAGE

# Seize the Moment, Share the Message

*And God Will Change Lives*

# Roberta Kuhne

MULTNOMAH BOOKS • SISTERS, OREGON

SEIZE THE MOMENT, SHARE THE MESSAGE
published by Multnomah Books
*a part of the Questar publishing family*

© 1995 by Roberta Kuhne

*International Standard Book Number: 0-88070-661-9*

Cover photo by David Hanover/Tony Stone Images
Cover design by David Uttley

Printed in the United States of America

Unless otherwise marked, Scripture quotations are from:
*The Holy Bible, New International Version* (NIV)
© 1973, 1984 by International Bible Society,
used by permission of Zondervan Publishing House

Scripture quotations marked NASB are from:
*New American Standard Bible*
© 1960, 1977 by the Lockman Foundation

95  96  97  98  99  00  01  02 — 10  9  8  7  6  5  4  3  2  1

*To my Robert*—
You are still the wind beneath my wings.

*To Brenda Desmaris and Terri Politan*—
You are my encouragers, prayer warriors,
and precious friends.

For as the rain and the snow come
down from heaven,
And do not return there without watering
the earth,
And making it bear and sprout,
And furnishing seed to the sower and
bread to the eater;
So shall My word be which goes
forth from My mouth;
It shall not return to Me empty,
Without accomplishing what I desire,
And without succeeding in the matter
for which I sent it.

ISAIAH 55:10–11, NASB

# Contents

# CHAPTER ONE

# HERE AM I, BUT SEND IN THE EVANGELIST

*"You will be my witnesses in Jerusalem, and in all Judea and Samaria, and to the ends of the earth."*

ACTS 1:8

I had my first experience with the gospel when I went back to college at age thirty-three. I was an art major and relished every moment of creative work. I would sit at my potter's wheel happily working with the clay and envisioning how my pot would soon equal an ancient Grecian urn or a vase from the Ming dynasty. I tend to dream big.

The potter next to me was a likable and friendly woman who participated in a weekly Bible study. However, she never talked about her faith or beliefs except when I would question her about the Bible study—questions like "Can't you read the Bible just once?" "Is it like a literature class?" "What's there to study?" "How can such an old book still be relevant today?" "When do you graduate from Bible study?"

With all my probing you would have expected her to invite me to her Bible study, right? But she didn't, and my curiosity finally got the best of me. So I announced to her one day, "I'm coming to your Bible study next week." With wide eyes and a stammering tongue she exclaimed, "You are?" "Yes," I said. The following Wednesday I attended my very first Stonecroft Ministry's Friendship Bible Coffee. Through this wonderful study I met my Savior, and my life has never been the same.

My friend was a godly Christian woman, but perhaps she felt inadequate or awkward in answering my questions. Perhaps she thought I was just being polite and making conversation. Maybe she didn't perceive my spiritually hungry heart. Possibly she lost sight of the fact I was facing a Christless eternity and needed help desperately. Or maybe she was scared to death to share the gospel. What if she didn't know the right things to say? What if I rejected the message or her? What if I asked, "What must I do to be saved?" What then? Perhaps she just wasn't sure what to do with the opportunity God was laying at her feet.

That's why I felt compelled to write this book. Many Christians who deeply love the Lord simply don't know where to begin with an unsaved person. We're scared. We feel ill equipped. We hate rejection. We're worried that people will think we're fanatics. We picture a wild-haired, poorly dressed man on a street corner, accosting all who pass by, waving his Bible and shouting, "Repent, repent!" That's probably not a picture of you. It's definitely not one of me. Whatever our insecurities and rationalizations, we end up thinking we should let the professionals do it anyway: "Lord, here am I, but send in the evangelist."

We're going to deal with all those concerns. You'll discover you don't have to be a raving evangelist to share Jesus Christ.

You'll discover this is a "Why, I can do that!" kind of book. It's an "I'm going to step out in faith" kind of book. We'll talk about key points to remember in witnessing and how to give our personal testimony—even a three-minute one—in a natural way. You'll learn how to be an effective witness for Jesus Christ in the arenas of life where God has placed you. Witnessing simply, naturally, and freely. Witnessing without fear.

Most of all I pray that God will use this book to ignite the embers in your heart, fan the flames of love, and give you a burden for the lost. Perhaps it will be through a story within these pages, a verse, or a quote. Surely our greatest motivation in life ought to be our desire that nonbelievers will come to know our great God. His love is limitless. His strength is enduring. His grace is lavish. His power is mighty. His mercy is impartial. His life is matchless. His tenderness is irresistible. And He is unforgettable. Now that's a God we can't help telling the world about.

### Every Life Is Important to God

We live just outside of Phoenix, Arizona. Before living in the desert I had always thought it was a pretty dry and desolate place—just thousands of miles of kitty litter! But I have grown to marvel at this wonderful place abundant with wildlife and wildflowers. One of my personal pleasures is the birds. From the first break of dawn over the mountains to the last of the reds and golds dripping from the setting sun, they are either singing and squawking or warbling and whistling, How I love these birds.

One afternoon I was having a quiet lunch, listening to my feathered friends squabbling, when—whack! A large dove flew into the window right in front of me. I gasped in horror because she hit it with full force. I prayed she would be all right. Of course she was just a bird, but God knows when even a sparrow falls from the sky, and He cares.

I walked over to her and saw that her neck was apparently broken. A lump rose in my throat, and my eyes began to well up with tears. Just a moment ago she was flying and free. Then she was gone. How quickly and unexpectedly life can be snuffed out!

It occurred to me, "That's just like some of my nonbeliever friends." They are flying along footloose and fancy-free when out of the blue—smack! A floor rapidly rises up to meet them in the face, or they fly into a wall at a dead run. How can we reach them for Christ before they breathe their last?

## We Are Called to the Rescue

Perhaps you're thinking, "What's with the 'we,' Roberta? I thought they were *your* friends." Ah, this is where you come in. We all have friends right outside our windows who hit a wall— they lose a job, face a divorce, deal with a rebellious child, contract a terminal illness—and who are lost. Paradise is lost if they never hear about the Savior. Maybe you're the one God wants to use to tell them.

I know you're all for people coming into a personal relationship with Jesus Christ or you wouldn't be reading this book. But maybe you're unsure of how it happens, when it happens, or even if you want to be there when it happens. We may have the same attitude toward witnessing that Woody Allen has toward death: "I'm not afraid to die. I just don't want to be there when it happens!" We'd like someone else to do the deed for us.

Within the pages of this book we'll see what it is like to be there "when it happens," when a life is transformed for Jesus Christ. We'll learn how it happens. Best of all, I believe we'll find ourselves eager to take advantage of even the smallest opportunities, ones we never noticed before. We can have a very real part in the salvation of others by just being who God made us.

I couldn't save that bird. All I could do was watch. But God has put us in a position to help save others. We must not sit and watch while they perish. We are not all evangelists—those who zealously preach the gospel—but we are all commanded to be *witnesses*, testifying to what we have seen and experienced.

Jesus told his apostles, "You will be my witnesses in Jerusalem, and in all Judea and Samaria, and to the ends of the earth" (Acts 1:8). Notice, Jesus said, "You *will* be." Not, "Here's a great idea!" "Consider this option." "If you feel like it, you can try it." No, Jesus commanded it.

Dear friends, this is not an option. This is either obedience or disobedience. This means love without limit, availability without being ashamed, and communication of truth without compromise. When we are disobedient to the commands of Christ, we are not in His will. It's really that simple. Where do you stand? Are you ready to be His witness?

Don't wait to be called as a missionary or preacher. We are being called right now, where we are living, working, and playing. We are being called from our easy chairs, our comfort zones, our complacency. Wherever life takes us, people will have already been prepared by the Holy Spirit, and they will be waiting. We will be in the right place at the right time for the God-arranged appointment.

## Lord, Where Do We Begin?

If the Statue of Liberty can beckon to the world, "Give us your tired, your poor, your huddled masses," then we should be willing to say to God, "Lord, we'll begin with whomever You give us." Give us the happy and the miserable, the slow and the hyper, the ugly and the pretty, the handsome and the haggard, the fit and the disabled, the blind and the lame. Give us the spiritually curious, the twice-a-year churchgoers, and the pew warmers who attend because it's a nice thing to do. Give us the homeless and the homebound, those who are far older than we and those much younger, the New Ager and the middle ager. Give us the ones who have dandruff in their hair, dirt under their fingernails, lice on their bodies, ragged clothes on their backs, and alcohol on their breath. Give us whomever You've got! And we'll tell them about Jesus, the unparalleled, unprecedented, unchangeable Savior.

Are these our words to the Lord? If the truth were known, we'd probably prefer the fit, the kind, the lovely, the educated, and the prosperous with whom to share Christ. Instead, let our cry be "Give us, O Lord, the ones who are weighted down with their sins and the ones who don't think they have any. The ones who are broken and don't know they can be made whole. The ones who think there are many ways to God, the ones who think they are God, and the ones who don't believe there is a God. Lord, give us whomever You've got, and that's where we'll begin."

## *I Made a Difference to That One!*

May we have the attitude of the small boy who had come down to comb the beach after the previous night's storm. All kinds of debris had washed up on the sand, but the young man's only concern was the hundreds, maybe thousands, of starfish stranded far from the water's edge.

The sun's rays were heating the small creatures as the boy worked frantically, throwing every starfish he could pick up back into the cool, life-giving water. An older gentlemen who had been watching him shook his head from side to side and said, "Son, it's foolish for you to take on this huge task. You aren't going to make any difference. There simply are too many."

The very young but very wise boy replied as he tossed yet another starfish into the water, "I'll bet it made a difference to that one, mister!"[1]

God used me recently to make a difference in one young waitress's life. Five of us were gathered in the lounge of a local resort hotel to say good-bye to our dear friend Sheryl who was moving to Fort Worth. Over cappuccino and a tray of sweets I was enthusiastically sharing my recent discovery in the book of Jeremiah. I chatted excitedly as the waitress served each of us. I thought as I watched her, "Hmm, maybe this beautiful young woman needs to hear about Jesus." (I'm a die-hard evangelist!) She watched us as we interacted, hugged, laughed, cried, prayed, and spoke freely about the Lord. This woman could see something in us that I believed she desired.

She took the first step, asking, "Where do you go to church?" Aha, there was the opening! We told her where we attended, and

I boldly invited her to a six-week class I was teaching at our church. I had no idea where she was spiritually, but I told her about the class and how the Word of God could help her. It wasn't difficult to discern she had a seeking, spiritually hungry heart since she was the one asking the questions.

That day I started praying for her salvation and for her to attend the class. And she came. One night several weeks into the series I closed with a prayer of surrender and dedication to Jesus. God had prepared her heart, and that night she trusted Christ.

God used us in a natural way to draw a lost, searching soul to Him because we weren't afraid to talk about Him in front of a stranger. If we had stopped our conversation every time she came to serve us, she might still be a nonbeliever.

### With Three You Have a Party

Let's each seek to make a difference in not just one life but at least three. The world will never be the same. And neither will we! May I present you with a challenge? After all, why take the time to read this book if it doesn't change things?

Right now, think of three people who need to hear the message of the gospel of Christ. Three lives that need to changed by believing in and receiving Jesus Christ. Three people who are hopelessly lost, apart from God. Three people who face a Christless eternity. Three people who long for peace and rest in their lives. Three people who need to know that there is One who will never leave them or forsake them. Three people who have tried to fill their lives with physical fitness, education, money, power, success, lovers, drugs, golf, bridge, crafts—you name it. But nothing ever satisfies apart from Jesus.

These are the ones our Lord seeks after. These are the ones He will place upon our hearts. May they be a burden we delight to carry. Who are these three in your life? Your neighbor, your sister-in-law, your golfing partner, the accountant in the next office, the salesperson who calls on you every month, the gardener, plumber, the nurse who cares for your mother, the woman in your aerobics class, your son's girlfriend, the sales clerk at the grocery store, the tailor who alters your suits, or the stranger you have yet to meet.

Ask God to show you whom to pray for, beginning now, in this chapter. Ask Him for opportunities, openings, and teachable moments. And in the following chapters we will look at a variety of ways to reach our "party of three" for Christ. But be prepared. Once we commit to pray for someone's salvation, things happen. God works deep in the heart and spirit of others in ways we cannot possibly fathom.

You might use this prayer:

Dear Father, I place (names) into Your loving hands, to draw into Your presence, and to believe in Your Son. May Your Holy Spirit convict, convert, comfort, and challenge each one as needed. Use me mightily in the process. Fill my mouth with the words to say and the wisdom to know when to say them. I depend on You to provide the opportunities for me to speak of You and the awareness to recognize them when they come. Give me ears to listen to their very real concerns and questions.

I pray for patience in the process. Give me a sincere love for (names) that You might communicate Your love to them through me. Use me, O God. I make myself wholly available for Your kingdom work. Thank You, Jesus, for the burden You have already put on my heart for (names). In Your powerful name, Jesus, I pray. Amen.

Your party of three is not a project or a few notches in your Bible. These people need to know you are their friend first; they are not part of a scheme we've concocted. Invite them to a sporting event, go out to lunch, play golf, tennis, or racquetball together. Spend a day at the zoo with all the children, help them shop for a special item, do a craft project, bake bread, or take an exercise class together. What do you enjoy doing that they might like? Invite them to share a small part of your life.

Let's give them what so few people will—our time, our hearts, our listening ears. I've discovered people will most often come to love us before they love our Savior. God's love must be evident in our witnessing. Be a friend—a loving, accepting, caring friend. Ask yourself, "How would Jesus act in this situation? How would He respond? How would He be a friend?"

It has been said, "A real friend warms you by his presence, trusts you with his secrets, and remembers you in his prayers." And "A friend is one who walks in when the rest of the world walks out."[2] Be there when the world walks out on your friend. He needs you most then. Be there to point him to the One who will walk alongside him in his darkest moments.

God is looking for available believers. "Preach the word; be ready in season and out of season" (2 Timothy 4:2, NASB). The verb translated "be ready" literally means "to stand by, to be available." We have been hand chosen by God to fulfill the Great Commission of Jesus Christ. My prayer is that you will indeed hear God speaking through the pages of this book and you'll say, "Here am I, Lord. I'm available, especially for my party of three. All the evangelists are busy right now anyway. Use me."

## HOOKS TO HANG YOUR HAT ON

- You have been chosen by God to be a witness for Jesus Christ.
  To be a witness is a command, not a suggestion.

- Be available, taking advantage of every opportunity
  to tell of Jesus' love and the hope that is in you.
What about the waitress at the coffee shop, your hairdresser
  or barber, your golfing buddy or tennis partner?

- Right now pray: "Lord, give me whomever You've got!"
  And be ready to receive whomever God sends your way.

- Remember the starfish story:
  "I'll bet it made a difference to that one!"
  Each life is important to God.
  Make a difference in someone's life this week.

- Pray daily for your party of three.

- Develop a friendship, not a project. Love them to Jesus.

## ALL THINGS CONSIDERED

1. What do you think is the greatest problem Christians have in witnessing (the Christian's problem, not the unbeliever's)? Specifically, how can this be overcome?

2. What is a witness in a court of law? What does he witness to? What questions does he answer the most?

3. Using a dictionary, define *evangelist* and *witness*. How is an evangelist different from a witness?

4. "And He said to them, 'Go into all the world and preach the gospel to all creation'" (Mark 16:15, NASB). To whom is Jesus commanding you to go? How are you able to accomplish this in "your world"? What are you going to do about it?

5. What do you think is the greatest need of men and women from God's point of view? What is the answer to that need? How would you communicate this to a nonbeliever?

6. Explain the following: reaching God, finding God, pleasing God, and knowing God. Which is the pathway to salvation?

7. What is the difference between being "religious" and having a "relationship with Jesus Christ"? (Use a dictionary to define *religious*.)

8. Write out a short paragraph explaining the gospel of Jesus Christ. Keep it simple but accurate and complete. The following verses will help you:

> "For all have sinned and fall short of the glory of God, and are justified freely by his grace through the redemption that came by Christ Jesus." (Romans 3:23–24)

"For the wages of sin is death, but the gift of God is eternal life in Christ Jesus our Lord." (Romans 6:23)

"I passed on to you as of first importance: that Christ died for our sins according to the Scriptures, that he was buried, that he was raised on the third day according to the Scriptures." (1 Corinthians 15:3–4)

"For it is by grace you have been saved, through faith—and this not from yourselves, it is the gift of God—not by works, so that no one can boast." (Ephesians 2:8–9)

9. Answer each of the following questions your nonbelieving friend just asked: Is the gospel laws, rules, and rituals? Is the gospel man-made ideas? Is the gospel anti-intellectual? Is the gospel blind faith?

# CHAPTER TWO

# BUT IT'S NOT MY GIFT

*Now concerning spiritual gifts, brethren, I do not want you to be unaware.*

1 CORINTHIANS 12:1, NASB

here was a time in my life when I simply couldn't understand why everyone wasn't like me. Wouldn't we get along much better if we were all happy, child-like, cheerful, fun loving, talkative, emotional, expressive, enthusiastic, and demonstrative, creating a thrill-a-minute environment at home? My temperament says, "If it isn't fun, why on earth do it?"

Why isn't the rest of humanity like me? Because the world would be in total chaos, that's why! Little would ever be accomplished (although we'd have a party in the process). We'd still be wandering around trying to figure out how to invent the wheel. Oh I would have created the concept with great enthusiasm but would have lost interest when someone told me to draw up the plans, find the materials, organize a work crew, and actually build the thing.

Then God brought some exciting information my way. I read *Personality Plus*[1] by Florence Littauer in which she discusses the four personality types: sanguine, choleric, melancholy, and phlegmatic. Through this book I came to understand the value of different personality types and the importance of knowing our temperaments in order to understand not only ourselves but others. This understanding is critical in learning to witness effectively, and therefore this overview of temperaments and spiritual gifts serves as a building block for the rest of the book.

Various systems for categorizing personality types exist, but for our purposes I will use the four temperament types just mentioned and also the DISC personality assessment system. This consists of the directive/determined style ("D"), the interactive/influencer ("I"), the supportive/soft-hearted ("S"), and the corrective/conscientious ("C"). Since we will not exhaust the subject of temperaments, I suggest you read a book such as Florence Littauer's *Personality Plus,* Tim LaHaye's *Why You Act the Way You Do,*[2] or Robert Rohm's *Positive Personality Profiles*[3] if you desire a more comprehensive study.

## The Way God Wired Us

God wired each of us with a unique personality before we were ever born, so it should be no surprise that we respond to various circumstances and people in amazingly different ways. We can learn to witness more effectively and naturally by understanding the strengths and weaknesses of our personality type and that of others, especially nonbelievers. Even a brief overview, as we have here, will help to maximize our potential in dealing with others.

Let's begin with the choleric or "D" (directive/determined) temperament. These people are independent, dominating, strong willed, goal oriented, self-sufficient, take-charge people. They make decisions based on logic rather than emotions. They are strong leaders, who hate to lose.

Once they set their minds on a goal it's quite difficult to change them. They often think their way is best, and it usually is because they have thought through the issues. This personality style swoops in and tells nonbelievers like it is: "Look, Jesus died for you, He is God, He forgives your sins. Repent and be saved or you're going straight to hell!" You might say this individual comes on a bit too strong. He is a bottom-line, net-it-out kind of person. The choleric/"D" needs encouragement to allow God to be in control, not his or her own well-thought-out, logical, no-nonsense plans. Although cholerics' methods may be good, God's way is always best.

The sanguine or the "I" (interactive/influencer) temperament is full of energy, exuberance, and enthusiasm. These people speak with animation and are usually fascinating storytellers. They are fun to be with and hardly ever lack for words. They usually have a strong ability to motivate others to their cause and are able to generate enthusiasm for their pet projects. But there are potential problems. They may talk with few intermissions or little evidence of coming up for air, so they can take over conversations without being aware of it. And their decisions are often based on emotions, which can run high and fast.

A sanguine/"I" might feel comfortable approaching a total stranger and in the course of five minutes delightfully direct the conversation toward spiritual matters. Making friends out of strangers is easy for them. But since they often would rather talk than listen, they need to learn to allow the nonbeliever to express his views and concerns. I call it "unpacking." Sanguines will never understand the nonbeliever's felt needs if they don't give him time to "unpack" what is on his mind. Sanguine/"I" personality types need to zip up. God will do the rest through them.

The melancholy or "C" (corrective/conscientious) temperament is task oriented, detail minded, analytical, introverted, perfectionistic, and self-sacrificing. Although these people can be moody, withdrawn, and even antagonistic, generally they are faithful friends and conscientious workers. They usually can be counted on to see a project to the end because of their strong desire to persist. Great works of art and music have been produced by this personality type.

The melancholy/"C" rehearses his presentation of the gospel until he has every detail down and in order. He loves the charts and graphs that explain the salvation message but may not recognize when a nonbeliever is ready to give his life to the Lord. He's often too busy analyzing every word in the conversation to see deep into the heart of the nonbeliever. And being a pessimist, he doubts he can lead someone to the Lord anyway. The melancholy/"C" personality needs to trust the Holy Spirit, for He will translate even the most carefully chosen words to the nonbeliever's heart in just the way he needs to hear them.

The phlegmatic or "S" (supportive/soft-hearted) is often considered the easiest person to get along with. Phlegmatics are likable, easygoing, calm, consistent, diplomatic, efficient, organized, nonconfrontational peacemakers. They don't usually seek positions of leadership but prove to be skillful leaders when the situation forces itself upon them. They are team players—devoted, loyal, and most cooperative.

This dear individual is perfectly content to watch the sanguine/"I" chatter, the melancholy/"C" rehearse the details of the gospel, and the choleric/"D" organize the group into "saved" and "going to hell." Phlegmatics are perfectly willing to spend time listening, nodding, and agreeing with the struggles of a nonbeliever but find it difficult to bring closure and ask, "Is there any reason you wouldn't trust your life to Christ right now?" The phlegmatic/"S" needs to learn to challenge the nonbeliever in holy boldness to make a decision after he's heard the truth.

Littauer's book really opened my eyes to see not only myself but others' personality traits as well. What freedom! After I learned this vital information, I began to appreciate several phlegmatic friends for being quiet, easygoing listeners, to accept the cholerics as generally wise decision makers, and to appreciate the melancholy people in my life without trying to change them into Holly Go Lightly characters.

As we desire to be better witnesses for Jesus, our knowledge of temperament traits will enlarge our avenues of communication and enable us to speak to the nonbelievers' felt needs. When we learn to "speak their language," it's amazing how much more productive our interaction with others can be. And a good place to begin is with a better understanding of ourselves and our party of three.

### The Holy Spirit Came Bearing Gifts

Before we can begin to understand how and where God wants to use us in witnessing, we need to find out what kind of equipment He's given us. So not only is it important to know our temperaments but also to discover and develop our spiritual gifts. It's time for an inventory of how God equipped us to minister.

When we first trusted Jesus as our Lord and Savior, the Holy Spirit came to take up permanent residence in us. He came as a gracious, invited guest bearing gifts—spiritual gifts that enable us to do the work of ministry. Every believer possesses at least one spiritual gift given by the Holy Spirit but usually more: "There are different kinds of gifts, but the same Spirit. There are different kinds of service, but the same Lord. There are different kinds of working, but the same God works all of them in all men.... All these are the work of one and the same Spirit, and he gives them to each one, just as he determines" (1 Corinthians 12:4–6, 11).

By identifying and developing our gifts, we fulfill God's plan for the Body of Christ and His plan for our lives. He has gifted each of us to make a unique and specific contribution to the church. Our spiritual gifts will be confirmed and affirmed through the Body of Christ as we exercise them.

Spiritual gifts are *not* natural talents and abilities that we possess from birth, nor are they secular areas in which we have been trained, but rather they are gifts bestowed at the time of salvation for the building up of the church. For those of you who may be discovering your gifts for the very first time, may you be as thrilled as I was to learn that God has a very special way for us to serve Him. And for those of you who may be thinking, "I already know this," have you seriously considered your spiritual gifts in the light of witnessing for Jesus Christ?

There are many spiritual gifts, but for our purposes we will discuss gifts that directly relate to witnessing because they are speaking gifts, service gifts, or people-intensive gifts—teaching, encouragement, evangelism, hospitality, leadership, mercy, prophecy, administration, giving, and helps.

Part of the responsibility of knowing our gifts is developing them. That doesn't mean we have to enroll in seminary, but we should ask the Lord to direct us to books, tapes, studies, people, and ministries that will help us to fulfill God's wonderful purpose for our lives. When we discover the spiritual gifts God has given us to use in a particular arena, we find fulfillment in our service.

To further your study and understanding of spiritual gifts, I recommend the books *Your Spiritual Gifts* by C. Peter Wagner[4] and *Spiritual Gifts and the Great Commission* by Edward F. Murphy,[5] along with *Network*,[6] a comprehensive study including a video, leader's manual, and assessment questionnaires. After my husband and I completed a four-week course in the *Network* study, we had little doubt as to our spiritual gifts. This excellent program was first developed through the ministry of Willow Creek Community Church of South Barrington, Illinois. The following information is taken from my own personal study and experience and these excellent sources.

## The Gift of Evangelism

This is the divine empowerment to share the gospel with nonbelievers in order to bring them to faith in Jesus and commitment to the Body of Christ (Ephesians 4:11).

Perhaps you're thinking, "That lets me off the hook. I don't have the gift!" Although evangelism is most definitely a spiritual gift and not all have that gift, we are all commanded by Jesus to be witnesses for Him to the unbelieving world. The evangelist Leighton Ford said, "We must not use the teaching of spiritual gifts as a cop-out to avoid our responsibility to share Christ with others. You may not be called as an evangelist, but you and every Christian, by an attitude of love, by compassionate concern, and by well-chosen words, can have the privilege to lead others... toward Jesus Christ."[7] Note the word *toward*. Not every one of us will lead others right into the waiting arms of Jesus at the moment of salvation, but all of us are able to lead others *toward* Christ.

The person with the gift of evangelism sees the chance, seizes the opportunity, and shares Christ. For example, last Christmas as I was shopping one afternoon, I decided I needed a cappuccino, badly. I walked into a coffee shop at the busiest time of day, but much to my surprise there was only the clerk and me. The young man waited on me and commented right out of the blue, "I really don't believe Christmas affects people in a religious sense, do you? It certainly hasn't affected me. It's parties, presents, and pigging out! Besides I'm not sure there is a God. How can we be sure anyhow? What do you think?" Was this a divine appointment or what? Talking about Jesus to people who might be willing to listen is my absolute favorite thing to do!

I told the young man, Jason, I was certain there was a God and that, in fact, I knew Him personally. "You do? Come on, how can you know God?" he asked. I told him we can know God through a personal relationship with Jesus Christ, that we can read about Jesus in the Gospel of John, and that Jesus claimed to be God so they crucified Him. "No kidding!" he said. As we talked for quite some time, I told him why Jesus died and that the greatest problem with humankind was sin. By the end of the conversation he said he would check out the Gospel of John as I suggested.

It was a very comfortable conversation. He asked the questions, I answered them. The person with the gift of evangelism senses the receptivity of the nonbeliever and seizes the moment to share the message. Actually we all can do that. It's just that people without the gift of evangelism may not recognize the opportunities the evangelist sees in every nook, cranny, and coffee shop.

While other spiritual gifts like encouragement and teaching may be respected by nonbelievers, I'm afraid we evangelists don't rate very high on the world's scale of admired individuals. Murphy Brown of television fame wanted to seek revenge on someone who had wronged her. She thought of any number of things to accomplish this, like dumping a load of fresh horse manure on her enemy's driveway or ordering a hundred pizzas to be delivered to the house. The deed had to be malicious and memorable. It had to have impact. Finally the perfect idea surfaced. "I'll call the local church and tell them I'm really interested in hearing about Jesus and could they please send over a couple of evangelists? Of course I'll give my 'friend's' address!" She could envision nothing worse than a couple of fire-breathing evangelists showing up at one's front door.

But we evangelists are a hardy lot. I guess God gave us an extra measure of boldness because He knew how the world would respond to us. Ask yourself: "Has God given me a burning desire to share my faith with unbelievers? Do I relish the opportunity to talk to others about Jesus? Do I find it easy to direct conversations to spiritual things? Do I see people come to a saving knowledge of Jesus Christ as a result?" If so, evangelism may be one of your spiritual gifts.

## The Gift of Teaching

Teaching is the divine empowerment to understand, clearly communicate, and give practical application of the Word of God to the lives of listeners (Romans 12:7; 1 Corinthians 12:28; Ephesians 4:11).

People with this gift have a passion to communicate, perhaps to nonbelievers, to children or college-age adults, to the divorced, or to single parents. It may be in one-on-one situations or large audiences. Some teach through their writings, some through radio and television. People with this gift love to study the Word of God and will spend long hours perfecting their understanding of Scripture and their presentation.

They are always teaching. In fact, many times teachers are eager to answer questions no one is asking! They're informed and can't wait to tell all the exciting things God has taught them. While the motivation is wonderful, some discretion needs to be exercised. I've discovered the average nonbeliever is not really interested in what a particular verb means in Greek. He wants to know what difference the Word of God will make in his life.

When guided by the Holy Spirit, teaching can be a powerful advantage in witnessing.

Ask yourself: "Do I love to study the Word of God for hours on end? Do I enjoy searching for illustrations and stories to make the material more meaningful? Am I excited and anxious to share what God has taught me from my study time? Do people enjoy listening to me? Do others in the Body of Christ affirm my gift? Is my teaching transforming lives?" If so, you likely have the gift of teaching.

## The Gift of Prophecy

Prophecy is the divine empowerment to proclaim, to cry out, to boldly announce the Word of God with power and clarity while applying its truth to everyday life situations (Romans 12:6).

The gift of prophecy is "forthtelling" (proclaiming) not fore-telling. Although this gift isn't predicting the future, people with this gift will be able to determine certain consequences of various behaviors and sins since they are students of the Word of God.

Those gifted in prophecy may appear authoritative and opinionated rather than compassionate. John the Baptist was such a man, and we know what happened to him. They are often politically minded and sensitive to social and moral trends in contemporary culture, and they boldly proclaim the Word of God regarding these. People with the gift of prophecy ensure that people with the gift of mercy have job security!

Those with the gift of prophecy often are used by God to convince nonbelievers of the error of their ways. Although they may have heard the gospel many times before, the bold proclamation of the Scriptures to their sinful state may be just the word they need to prompt that final step of faith.

Ask yourself: "Do I boldly proclaim the Word of God to bring about repentance and correction? Am I politically minded? Do I speak on today's social ills from a biblical viewpoint? Do I clearly and powerfully present God's truth? Have nonbelievers repented and turned from their sinful ways as a result? Is the Body of Christ edified by my words?" If you have this gift, you will need frequent and long periods of time alone with the Lord in His Word. If you are truly yielded to Christ, He will use you in a mighty way to witness for the Kingdom.

## *The Gift of Encouragement*

Encouragement is the divine empowerment to give hope and confidence, and to strengthen and affirm those who are hurting (Romans 12:8).

People with the spiritual gift of encouragement often make wonderful counselors. My friend Cathy Schadt has this special gift. She is continually drawn to hurting people in order to build them up, and they in turn are pulled to her like a gigantic magnet. She listens intently, nurtures hope in needy hearts, and sees potential in their future. Cathy will spend quality time with nonbelievers to develop meaningful friendships. She then will comfort and give wise counsel, waiting for just the right time to weave in the saving power of Jesus Christ regarding their dilemma.

Ask yourself: "Am I drawn to people who are discouraged and need affirmation and a supportive voice? Do I see potential in others? Am I able to communicate that to them? Do they find hope in their time with me?" If the answer is yes, you may have this very special gift, and nonbelievers will find a receptive, listening heart in you.

## The Gift of Hospitality

Hospitality is the divine empowerment to offer an open, welcoming house and warm heart by providing food, lodging, and fellowship (1 Peter 4:9–10).

Hospitality is a wonderful gift that can exhibit itself through hosting Bible studies, reaching out to the neighborhood, or opening one's home to those in need. Those who possess this gift provide an environment for the unsaved to feel accepted and comfortable in the presence of believers. This is such an important gift we will discuss it in greater detail in the "True Life of the Party" chapter.

People with this gift are not overly concerned with the condition of their home but are deeply interested in the care and comfort of their guests. Now I love to entertain, have house guests, and host dinner parties. But my pride gets in the way, and I want everything in its place and our home looking its best. I don't want to let guests in the front door unless I have gardenias floating in the toilets! That's not the gift of hospitality.

Ask yourself: "Am I always eager to receive guests, regardless of the condition of my home? Does hospitality come before my pride? Do I delight in providing food and comfort for guests or those in need? Am I a lover of strangers for the glory of God?" If so, then hospitality may be one of your spiritual gifts.

## The Gift of Leadership

This is the divine empowerment to lead, set goals, and motivate people to work harmoniously together for God's purposes (Romans 12:8).

Those with the gift of leadership love to dream big dreams for God. They are intense, well disciplined, and good at delegation. Gifted leaders do not manipulate or coerce their followers; their followers enjoy being led. Those with the gift of leadership are confident people who know where they are going and who take the steps necessary to get there.

A gifted leader can be a powerful force in organizing and developing events, ministries, and opportunities for evangelistic outreach. A person with this gift will often be the one who motivates others to develop small group Bible studies throughout an entire city or organizes a luncheon or seminar to present the gospel to nonbelievers. This spiritual gift is yet another way to lead nonbelievers *toward* Jesus Christ. Gifted leaders who are in the forefront of ministries are subject to greater scrutiny and are often looked to as models of Christian behavior.

Chuck Colson has the gift of leadership. He launched the Prison Fellowship ministry in 1976 as a leadership and discipleship training course for Christian inmates. Today it is a multifaceted ministry with over forty thousand volunteers. Thousands have been won for Christ as a result of Colson's spiritual gifts being used for the Body of Christ.

Ask yourself: "Do my leadership skills generate confidence in followers? Do people voluntarily work together under my leadership? Am I a good delegator of responsibilities? Am I disciplined? Am I confident of where I am going in my leadership capacity?

BUT IT'S NOT MY GIFT

Do I love the role of providing leadership?" If the answers are yes, then you have the spiritual gift of leadership.

## The Gift of Mercy

Mercy is the divine empowerment to have empathy and compassion for individuals suffering from physical, mental, or emotional problems and to minister lovingly and happily to alleviate their suffering (Romans 12:8).

We are all called to be merciful, but people specifically gifted with mercy manifest compassion and kindness as a lifestyle. These precious individuals don't just react to suffering people; they seek out opportunities to show kindness and to demonstrate love for even the most wretched. God has provided the person gifted in mercy wonderful ways in which to witness for Him.

Mother Teresa is such an individual. She and her band of dedicated women search the streets, the alleys, and the garbage dumps of life to rescue and comfort the sick, the dying, and the disabled in the name of Christ.

Ask yourself: "Do I cheerfully and appropriately reach out to people who are suffering? Do I seek out those who need help and develop a personal ministry with them? Can I spot hurting people before most others do? Do I manifest my gift by ministering in the name of Jesus Christ to those who are suffering?" If you have this gift, you are indeed a blessing to the Body of Christ and a true comfort and witness to the nonbeliever.

## The Gift of Administration

Administration is the divine empowerment to understand, execute, and plan for functions and goals within the Body of Christ (1 Corinthians 12:28).

The word for *administration* in the Greek text is the word for *helmsman*, the person in charge of the detail work in guiding the ship to its destination. The person with the gift of administration differs from the one with the gift of leadership. While the leader is like the captain of a ship, the one gifted in administration stands between the "captain" and the "crew," overseeing the business matters of a ministry, interfacing with the staff, and checking details.

When I served as Teaching Director of Community Bible Study, one of the important functions was to manage, coordinate, and administrate the details of the ministry. This was clearly not my gift. So my dear friend Kathy Riffer became the coordinator. She loved all the details which drove me crazy. She ordered materials, kept records, organized files, maintained a ministry checkbook, and generally saw to it that we reached our destination. Not only that, but she had fun doing it! How I thanked God for her. A person with the gift of administration frees up others in the ministry to exercise their gifts.

People with this gift interface with many nonbelievers in the business processes of a ministry. The administrator may not be the one who leads nonbelievers into a prayer for salvation, but he or she can lead them *toward* Christ by inviting them to an outreach function of the ministry. Here is a wonderful opportunity to model Christian character in the midst of "doing business."

Ask yourself: "Do I have a love of detail to accomplish the goals of ministry? Am I able to devise and execute effective plans for realizing these goals? Do I find satisfaction in organizing, arranging, systematizing, and coordinating the work of ministry and doing it for the glory of God?" If so, your gift may be to serve at the helm.

## The Gift of Giving

This is the divine empowerment to contribute material and financial resources liberally and cheerfully to the work of the Lord (Romans 12:8).

We all are called to give a portion of our income to the Lord whether we are rich or poor. But those with the gift of giving have an attitude of "It's not how much of my money I give to God, but rather how much of God's money I keep."

Often those with the gift of giving are successful, affluent people. God may have seen fit to bless them with abilities that enable them to exercise this gift better. Those with more limited resources may be quite creative in their giving, freely and joyfully offering their furniture, clothes, food, books, time, or whatever is needed. Those gifted in giving can purchase Bibles and can contribute to evangelistic ministries and outreach events for nonbelievers, thus releasing their resources for the spread of the gospel.

Joan and Jerry Colangelo have been blessed with financial resources to exercise their gift of giving in unique ways. In his high-profile position as president of the Phoenix Suns, Jerry has accomplished much for the Lord.

Joan has also exercised her gift. One year she hosted a Christmas tea at the Ritz-Carlton ballroom. Each Christian woman invited was to fill her assigned table with nonbelievers. Women from this community were abuzz with excitement and most anxious to attend. Some may have come just to see and be seen at the event, but as you know, God will use whatever it takes to bring people to Himself.

Ann Graham Lotz, Billy Graham's daughter, spoke and presented the gospel to about five hundred women. A follow-up Bible study was then offered for those interested. Women were given the opportunity to hear the good news of Jesus Christ and enjoy a lovely tea as the guest of Joan Colangelo, and lives were changed as a result of her gift of giving.

Ask yourself: "Do I look for ways to give my financial and material resources for the work of the Lord? Do I give cheerfully and liberally as I am led by the Lord? Has God blessed me with resources that enable me to exercise this gift freely?" Perhaps you have the gift of giving.

## The Gift of Helps

The gift of helps is the divine empowerment to accomplish physical tasks which are required for the life and ministry in the Body of Christ (1 Corinthians 12:28).

I'm convinced that ministries and churches would fall apart were it not for people with the gift of helps—the behind-the-scenes people who enable others to exercise their gifts. Those with the gift of helps make the coffee, serve the cookies, set up the chairs, and clean up the mess when it's over. Church secretaries or ministry administrative assistants often possess the gift of helps, freeing up pastors, teachers, and leaders for their ministries.

Whenever we have an event at our church, I see the same women in the kitchen. At the last event I noticed them because I came into the kitchen to find a paper napkin on which to illustrate the salvation message to someone. When I entered, it was obvious they needed help preparing the dinner. I wanted to exit quickly. After all, I didn't want to get in their way! Although I don't have the gift of helps, it certainly doesn't excuse me from helping. I did help that evening with the preparation and the cleanup, but let me tell you, it was not my heart's delight to wash two hundred sticky dishes.

That's the difference. People with the gift of helps, who are so often behind the scenes in the kitchens and offices, truly enjoy their labors and attach spiritual value to them. It's satisfying to these people to set up for an event or project and then clean it up or take it down. They talk, laugh, and have a wonderful time. If we were to ask, they would tell us, "I am doing this for the glory of God. I love my work."

In the area of witnessing, those gifted in helps will be the first to see a physical need in a situation or another person. They are at the nonbeliever's home providing meals, offering to baby-sit, organizing a carpool for a sick mother, cleaning the house, or doing the laundry. They are in the workplace volunteering for tasks that will make another's job easier. They are witnesses for Christ even as they sit at their computers, make copies of documents for a coworker, take notes at a staff meeting, or volunteer to set up for a conference. Their servant hearts cause nonbelievers to wonder and at times to ask why they do what they do. Those with the gift of helps can lead others *toward* Christ.

Ask yourself: "Am I always looking to see what needs to be done in my church or ministry and then do it? Do I see the spiritual impact of my giftedness? Do I delight in accomplishing physical tasks to free others up to exercise their spiritual gifts?" Then you may have the wonderful gift of helps. If so, you are a cherished saint to the Body of Christ. You are of inestimable worth!

### Discover God's Purpose for Your Life

It wasn't until I discovered my spiritual gifts and worked at developing them that I could say with certainty, "I know God's purpose for my life. I know the ministry He is calling me to. I strongly sense the goals He is seeking to accomplish through me. I am delighted with the passion He has given me for certain ministries. And I love the work He has gifted me to do."

That's how it is. God has gifted and empowered every member of His church to be personally fulfilled by a ministry. When you discover how God has made you and gifted you and what your passion is, you will delight in your work because that's what God created you to do. Ask God to use you in all your uniqueness to seek and save the lost. While it is the Lord, of course, who seeks and saves, we are privileged to serve in the process.

---

**HOOKS TO HANG YOUR HAT ON**

- Begin this week to read about the various temperaments from the recommended sources.

- Seek to identify the temperaments of your household members and friends.

- Identify and study the temperaments of your party of three.

• Write down three personality characteristics
of each of your party of three.
Consider how you might reach out to each of them in light of
their temperament differences.

• Ask a close friend to help you identify your spiritual gifts.
Help your friend identify his or her gifts.
Review the list together of those gifts covered in this chapter.

• Identify and use at least one of your spiritual gifts this week.
Be mindful of doing this as a witness for Jesus Christ.

## ALL THINGS CONSIDERED

1. The sanguine/"I" temperament is talkative and enthusiastic. The choleric/"D" is strong willed, decisive, and independent. The melancholy/"C" is analytical, introverted, and a perfectionist. The phlegmatic/"S" is easygoing, likable, and efficient. In what ways might each of these individuals use his or her personality traits to reach nonbelievers? How can the weaknesses in these temperaments be a problem?

2. "So I say, live by the Spirit, and you will not gratify the desires of the sinful nature. For the sinful nature desires what is contrary to the Spirit, and the Spirit what is contrary to the sinful nature.... Those who belong to Christ Jesus have crucified the sinful nature with its passions and desires" (Galatians 5:16–17, 24). How can the weaknesses in our temperaments become our strengths? In what ways will understanding this help us in sharing the gospel?

3. Why would we bother learning the temperaments of nonbelievers when truth is truth, no matter how we present the

gospel? To understand this better, think of a time you heard two sermons on the same scriptures but one sermon barely kept you awake while the other held you on the edge of your seat. What made the difference to you? How can understanding your friends' personalities help you make a difference with them for Christ?

4. Describe the distinction between natural talents and spiritual gifts. When are they received? Whom do they edify?

5. What is the difference between a teacher at a school and a person gifted in teaching the Scriptures? Do they both have the spiritual gift of teaching? Does a person who enjoys giving his resources to worthy community causes have the spiritual gift of giving? What is the difference, if any?

6. Think of one Christian who has made a profound mark in your life, perhaps the one who led you to Christ. Describe one or more of the spiritual gifts he or she exercised in leading you toward Christ or presenting the gospel.

7. What is the difference between someone who is a witness for Jesus Christ and someone with the spiritual gift of evangelism? How are they alike? Name at least one person you know with the gift of evangelism.

8. How might a person spiritually gifted in prophecy present the gospel differently than someone gifted with mercy?

9. If the person with the gift of encouragement wins nonbelievers over by words of love, how does the individual with the gift of mercy win them over?

10. Have you ever had an opportune moment to share Christ? What happened? If you blew it, were you able to "seize the moment" at a later time?

# CHAPTER THREE

# FISHERS OF SOULS

*"Come, follow me," Jesus said, "and I will make you fishers of men."*

MARK 1:17

The moment had finally come for me. I was all decked out in waders, felt boots, and my fishing hat, and was standing waist deep in the Clark Fork River just outside of Missoula, Montana. It was early evening; the sun had bedded down behind the mountains and pulled a blanket of stars over its head. The river was quiet except for the trout that were beginning to rise out of the water and catch the stonefly hatch. I felt as if I were starring in *A River Runs through It*.

For months I had studied, practiced, and outfitted for this magnificent sport of fly-fishing. Now I was finally in the river with real live fish. I raised my rod and executed my first cast. It was a terrible presentation, but I actually had a strike! After netting the little guy, however, I knew I simply couldn't keep such a youngster and ever sleep peacefully again. So I released him to grow into a teenager for next year's catch.

Although I'm a total novice at fly-fishing, I'm definitely hooked on it. It is so beautiful to participate in and watch. The artistic grace of a perfect cast reminds me of water ballet. The soft whisper of the line as I draw a pattern in the sky is quieting to my soul. And there's something almost mystical about wading in the river with the fish, about entering their world.

But I had a greater purpose for learning to fly-fish than mere pleasure. I believed I could gain insight into what Jesus meant when he said we were to be fishers of men. And indeed I did. My summer experience in the cool rivers of Montana cemented the truth in my mind that we must become students of the "fish" and learn well the art of "fishing" if we are going to obey the Lord's command to be fishers of men's souls. And the place we must begin is stepping into the water where the fish live.

### *Fishermen Get in the Water*

A dear and special Christian friend of mine, Sue Hunter, actively takes the gospel message to nonbelievers, right where they live. And she prays for God to bring someone new into her path. Sue told me the following story of one of her "fishing excursions."

"I was dashing through the 'sea of cosmetics' at one of my favorite department stores when a special promotion caught the corner of my eye. With the purchase of a certain amount of product you could receive a professional 8″ x 10″ photo, plus a makeover. I had been doing my Christmas shopping. You know what that's like. So I thought as I looked at the glamour photos, 'It's time to do something for me.' Without hesitation I made an appointment. Trust me, God was in this.

"My makeover day soon arrived. First the makeup artist got her hands on me, then the hair stylist, and finally the professional photographer. No question about it. The woman I saw in the mirror was ravishing! The photographer had a rack of clothes to try on for the photos, items like velvet jackets, sequined tops, and ostrich boas—just the sort of things I normally wear cleaning out the litter box. The photographer introduced herself by saying, 'I'm Penny. I'm going to take your picture today, and I'm going to make you look smashing!' Right away I liked her. This was my kind of woman.

"I noticed the necklace she was wearing and said, 'Penny, I've been admiring the gold cross you have.' She put her hand to her chest, saying, 'I just can't get through a day without this.' 'Oh really?' I replied. 'This sounds as if it is very important to you.' 'It truly is,' she said. 'I can't tell you how important.' I pursued it further, saying, 'It's very important in my life as well.' Penny asked, 'Do you go to church?' 'Yes I do,' I answered. 'Do you?' 'Well yes,' she said, 'but they don't study the Bible enough.' Lights flashed inside my head, bells rang, and a host of angels sang 'Alleluia!' I wondered, 'Lord, could this be what I have prayed and prepared myself for?' Penny said, 'Maybe I should visit your church. There are so many things I don't understand about the Bible.'

"This is where you get the net ready because the fish is already jumping into the boat! I'm an eager fisher of souls, so I said, 'Years ago I didn't understand spiritual things very well either. Someone took me under her wing and spent time studying the Bible with me. I've always felt a responsibility to pass that opportunity on to others.'

"Penny responded, 'I'd like to do something like that. Who do you think I could do that with?' I thought, 'What about the smashing woman in front of your camera?' So I asked, 'How about me?' 'Great,' she said. 'I'm free Monday.' I was thinking, 'It's just a few weeks before Christmas. I have to be half-crazed to start a study now!' But I could see God's hand upon her.

"At first we met for our Bible study in a shopping mall food court over coffee. Later we decided to meet at Penny's home, so I was meeting her where she lived—literally. She was a sponge and just couldn't get enough of the Word. One day I asked her, 'Is there any reason you wouldn't make a decision to trust Christ?'

"'I've already made the decision,' she said. 'But why did He have to die such a horrible death? What did He really do for me on the cross? What was the connection between God and Jesus?' Her questions forced me to go back to the basics of my faith. I kept simplifying the message and presenting the simple truth of the gospel: 'Christ died for our sins as substitution for us on the cross. We deserved death, but He took our sins upon Himself. He was buried, rose again, and now lives in the hearts of those who place their trust in Him.' Then that glorious day arrived when she said, 'I've decided to make Jesus the Lord of my life.' I told you God was in this!"

Jesus died for the worth of a Penny. She was no ordinary penny but was of inestimable worth to Jesus, and He couldn't bear to spend eternity without her. Sue was a fisher of souls that God used to reach into the waters and bring Living Water to this precious one.

LESSON NUMBER ONE FOR FISHERS OF SOULS: We need to go where nonbelievers live, work, and play.

## Match the Hatch

In the fly-fishing world it's important to "match the hatch." When insects hatch from their nymph stage in the water to their adult flying stage, they all seem to hatch at once. The river virtually churns as the fish rise to catch the flying insects. Good fishermen will observe what the fish are biting, and they will search their fly collections to try to match the hatch.

As I observed this, I couldn't help but think, "This is what we need to do—match the hatch." Translated this means we should meet nonbelievers at their point of need. What are they hungry for? People are not likely to listen to the gospel message unless they see that it addresses their needs, and every human need is matched by some aspect of the gospel of Jesus Christ. While their greatest need is for repentance and forgiveness of their sins, each person will have a different aspect of his or her sin problem to deal with. We don't want to present Jesus as the "cosmic fixer of all ills," but we do want to share how He will be with them in their times of crisis, providing comfort, wisdom, and love.

When people's needs are great, when they are in a time of crisis, they are often more open to the gospel. They may be struggling with a failing marriage, loss of a job, a wayward child, a debilitating illness, a financial crisis, or a destructive habit. Though the marriage may still fail and the disease not be cured, Jesus can give them peace in the midst of such personal turmoil. They need to know that a personal relationship with Jesus Christ is the all-important step in dealing with the dilemmas of life.

Chuck Swindoll tells a story about a woman who was grieving over the death of her husband. For weeks she went to the grave site and talked to the marble tombstone where he was buried.

Swindoll's mother happened to be at the cemetery one day and went over to comfort the woman. She told her about Jesus Christ, simply, purely, and with conviction. The grieving woman heard Jesus was the answer to her loneliness, her emptiness, and her loss. Her heart was open and tender. Her need was obvious. And she made a decision to trust Jesus for her life and eternal destiny.

The widow then decided on a graveyard ministry. She was a new believer, and nobody told her it probably wouldn't be a fruitful ministry. So she spent her weekends at the cemetery ministering to those who were grieving and were talking to tombstones as she had once done. She led hundreds of people to life in Jesus Christ while walking among the dead.

We need to keep the unbeliever's personal situation in mind. What about a young woman who has been criticized by her family all her life? Maybe she never received love or approval unless performance standards were met. Perhaps her family or significant others were always judging her. How should we present Jesus to her? More judgment? More condemnation?

What she needs to hear is that she matters to God and He loves her unconditionally. He has set His heart upon her. He will pursue her as a relentless lover searching after His beloved. His irresistible love will woo her to Himself. Those who have never known the commitment, devotion, and faithfulness of a loving relationship hunger for such a love. Let them know Jesus is the ultimate lover, and tell what He did in the name of love.

Others desperately need to hear of His complete forgiveness of their sins. Some need to know they have not committed the unforgivable sin. I knew of a young couple who had committed adultery. They went to see a pastor because they were seekers of God but didn't know quite what they were looking for. Somewhere in the conversation they perceived that the pastor said they had committed the unforgivable sin. Rather than hearing the gospel and the grace of forgiveness, they left condemned. The pastor may not have used the words "unforgivable sin," but his language fueled that belief. They eventually came to know Jesus but not before making serious detours in their spiritual journey.

A young, disabled woman shared with me that she would like very much to give her life to Jesus but she had committed an unforgivable sin. "So, you think your sin is bigger than God?" I asked. "It must be pretty bad! Are you saying that Jesus' death on the cross for the sins of the world didn't cover yours?" She prayed to receive Christ that afternoon.

Many people are certain that, because of the lives they have led, the evil they have done, and the people they have hurt, they cannot be forgiven by God. They are convinced God is just too angry. We can communicate the gospel to them by assuring them of the boundless forgiveness and mercy of our wonderful Lord.

Then there are people—the arrogant, the hard of heart, the prideful—who need to realize judgment is coming. They have sinned greatly. They deserve eternal death, banishment from God forever. More than the tender, soft-hearted, or the humble, they need to hear the message of judgment. Yet there is a way of escape; Jesus has provided a way.

What are we to do? Stop. Look. Listen. Pray. Stop long enough to determine where nonbelievers are spiritually. God will often bring across our paths people with whom we can identify. Look closely at the condition of their hearts and minds. Listen to them carefully. Listen to their hurts, their wounds, their needs. Listen to their words, spoken and unspoken. Then pray for wisdom, insight, and discernment to meet their needs with the message of the good news.

LESSON NUMBER TWO: Look for hungry, receptive nonbelievers—in all places—and meet them at their point of need with the grace of the gospel of Jesus Christ.

## *Prepare for the Presentation*

For the fisherman the "presentation" of the lure or bait is most important since fish will often ignore the bait if it plops, plunges, or plummets unnaturally. In fact, any unexpected or unfamiliar shapes can quickly scare them off and send them into holding lanes, which is called "refusal."

My fly-fishing presentations weren't so hot; in fact they just noisily plopped into the river. My line dragged, rippling the water, until every trout within miles was no doubt laughing hysterically. By my second night of fishing, the word had spread in the underwater trout world, and we didn't catch a thing. Well, except for the wooden log I enthusiastically hauled in. That must be why they call it "fishing" not "catching."

But it did remind me of the importance of presentation in fishing for souls. As Scripture says, "Always be prepared to give an answer to everyone who asks you to give the reason for the hope that you have. But do this with gentleness and respect" (1 Peter 3:15). Fishers of men need to be prepared so they can execute carefully the presentation of the message. Some will refuse God's transforming message for now and go back into their "holding lanes." But a fisher of men has an attitude of expectancy as he or she strives to exercise patience and waits for the next opportunity.

Bill Hybels has certainly prepared his "presentation" of the message. In a sermon Bill told about a time he and his wife, Lynne, were sailing in the Caribbean. Just after anchoring for the day, they received an invitation to a cocktail party on another boat and went. Nobody knew anyone else, so as is often the case, especially with men, the conversation opened with, "What do you do?" Bill stood with a Perrier in his hand, knowing he would have to use the p word. "I'm a pastor," he said. The replies went something like "Oh," "That's nice," "Oh really?" and "How interesting." The evening went along remarkably well, considering there was a "man of the cloth" on board.

When it came time for Bill and Lynne to go back to their boat, Lynne climbed into the dinghy first. Then just as Bill had one foot on the ladder and one in the dinghy and the dinghy began to float away, a woman called out to him, "By the way, what is a Christian anyway?" This fisher of souls had about thirty seconds to seize the opportunity before he would fall into the drink or the dinghy.

Bill replied, "Well, it's different from religion. Religion is spelled *Do*—what we try to do to get to God. Christianity is spelled *Done*; God has already done everything we need to get to heaven." Into the dinghy he went, and they were off. Revival broke out, everyone fell to their knees, and they threw all their liquor overboard! Okay so it didn't happen, but the point is Bill was prepared.

Put yourself in that situation. What would you have said? In my early Christian days I would have said something like, "In the beginning there was creation. Well, actually God was in the beginning; creation came later. Then there were all these animal sacrifices, but they didn't really do anything. There had to be a real sacrifice. You see Micah predicted Jesus' birth years before He was born. Oh and did I tell you He's going to come again? Ah…would you like to surrender your life to Jesus now?" By that time if I hadn't already fallen into the water, they might have thrown me in, calling out, "Religious fanatic overboard! By the way, who's Micah?" I simply hadn't prepared myself to explain the hope that was in me.

But now I am prepared, and you can be too. Occasionally nonbelievers will say to me, "I'm just not into religion like you are." They are often startled by my reply: "You know, I'm not into religion either because it's a dead-end road." Then I share the following with them. "Religion is spelled *Do*. It is human effort trying to gain God's approval, to earn heaven, to make up for past sins. The problem with doing these things is you never know if you've done enough. You haven't been told the quota. How much is enough?" Ask your nonbelieving friend, "Would a loving, righteous God play games with us, telling us to do all kinds of good works but never telling us when we've done enough?"

I go on to explain, "Christianity is spelled *Done.* Since we can never save ourselves by doing good works or being good enough, Jesus did something for us we couldn't do for ourselves. He died in our place—the sinless One for the sinners. When He died for our sins, He said, 'It is finished.' That means done, completed, finalized. There is no more to be done but to place your trust in what Christ did for you. Good works will then be the natural outflow of your new life, not a requirement to earn heaven.

"Christianity is not a religion. It is a relationship with the person of Jesus Christ. Religions consist of humanity's efforts to reach up to God. Christianity is totally different. God reached down to rescue mankind."

These may be just the words a nonbeliever needs to hear some day when you're between the dinghy and the deep blue sea!

## Prepare Your Own Story

One easy way to give an account of the hope that is in you is to tell your own story, your testimony, your spiritual journey into the heart of Jesus.

Here's an example of a person's testimony that takes less than a minute: "For the first thirty-two years of my life I thought I was a Christian, but I wasn't. I had been baptized and even went through confirmation. I attended church occasionally. I sincerely tried to live a moral life, but a few years ago I discovered what a real Christian was, and I became one. If you'd ever be interested in how it happened, I'd be happy to tell you. It's been the greatest decision of my life."

For nonbelievers this is a nonthreatening, nonaccusatory, nonpreachy approach that helps them to reflect on their own lives. You've also left the ball in their court by saying, "If you'd ever be interested, I'd be happy to tell you how I became a Christian." Then wait for the Holy Spirit to prepare their hearts.

Be prepared for your "fishing excursion" with your testimony. Since it's your own life, it shouldn't be difficult to remember, but you need to organize it in your mind. I suggest writing it out. One good approach is to create an outline with three parts: What were you like before Christ? How did you come into a personal relationship with Jesus? What is different about your life today?

Before you begin, ask the Lord to direct your thoughts and to give you wisdom and discernment to know what you should share about your life. Bear in mind, we don't need to give every lurid detail of our B. C. (Before Christ) days. I'd skip the "Wait till I tell what I used to do!" details. That is not glorifying to God.

Be clear about how you first trusted Christ. This is a perfect place to present the gospel: Christ died for our sins, He was buried, He was raised on the third day, He was seen by many. And so what did you do? You trusted Christ. Tell them how Jesus met you at your point of need.

Now the best part. Why are you so different today? How are your hopes, plans, dreams, motives, values, desires, and priorities different from before? Tell them what your life is like today. How is Jesus changing you?

Now that you have your three-point outline in mind, do it in three minutes. That will quickly cut away many of the rabbit trails we take others down as we tell them about our spiritual journey.

## Getting Down to the Basics

When that golden moment does arrive in which nonbelievers are ready to listen, we need to give them the simple, plain message of the gospel. Nonbelievers usually think they already know all they need to about Christianity. And many believe they are Christians. After all they were born in America, went to Sunday school, were baptized, and maybe were even confirmed. They also think they understand what to do to get to heaven: "Be good. Go to church. Quit drinking, swearing, and fooling around."

The problem is, of course, they haven't gotten the message right. And little wonder. They have heard, "You must make a commitment, you must give your life, you must receive a life, you must invite a life, you must dedicate your life, you must exchange a life, you must surrender your life, you must say 'the prayer.'" No wonder they're confused. That's not the gospel.

The gospel of Jesus Christ is clearly presented in 1 Corinthians 15:2–6. Paul tells us, "By this gospel you are saved" (15:2). Here is the simple message of the gospel: "Christ died for our sins" (15:3), "he was buried" (15:4), "he was raised on the third day" (15:4), and "he appeared to more than five hundred of the brothers" (15:6). Simple, concise, to the point.

And if our non-Christian friends reply, "Oh I already know that, but what do I do about it?" You can respond to them with John 3:16: "For God so loved the world that he gave his one and only Son, that whoever believes in him shall not perish but have eternal life." They need to trust Christ as their Savior. The Amplified Bible says, "whoever believes in (trusts in, clings to, relies on)." The real issue is to trust in His death on the cross for our sins. The one and only thing that will gain us heaven is Jesus Christ.

Andy Stanley said it so well in one of his sermons: "Becoming a Christian isn't promising something to God. It's taking advantage of a promise. It isn't about giving something to God. It's about receiving something. It isn't about making a commitment. It's about taking advantage of a commitment made to us."

It's a two-thousand-year-old message, yet it is still life transforming for today's man and woman. It's beautiful, breathtaking, and blessed good news.

LESSON NUMBER THREE: Be prepared. Train for and practice presenting the gospel so you don't scare the nonbeliever away. Become skilled in telling your own story.

### *Fishers of Souls Show Patience and Perseverance*

When a fisherman sets out in the early morning with his gear all packed, rods ready, and flies tied, anticipation is high. But he is prepared to work through the process of fishing with patience. Very seldom do seasoned fisherman become stressed out, over-anxious, and frazzled at the thought of fishing. Fishing requires perseverance and patience. Fishing could even be called waiting!

Witnessing also is a process of perseverance and patience—the two big Ps. The process of bringing a person to the point of salvation may take weeks, months, or even years, and the nonbeliever may have heard the gospel many times over. But if we're patient and we persevere, then perhaps he will one day say, "Oh I get it now. Jesus died for my sins so I could get to heaven," as you're thinking, "That's what I've been saying for six months!"

My sister Pam is a beautiful Christian woman. I trusted Christ several years before she did, so she frequently reminds me I'm her older sister in more ways than one. When I first became a Christian, I lived in Hillsborough, California, and she lived in Naperville, Illinois. We often talked long distance as the minutes clicked by. With my limited knowledge as a baby Christian, I would give her the gospel in every creative way possible. I'd go on and on, thinking the more I said the better she would understand.

You know what she would do? As she was cooking, she would set the phone on the counter, stir the pot, wash the lettuce, or cut up the onions. Here I was, resting on the counter going, "Yak, yak, yak, blah blah, blah, are you listening?" She'd pick up the receiver and say, "Uh huh," then go back to peeling the potatoes. She confessed this to me much later when I was strong enough to handle it.

But through those years I was patient, and I persevered, and I prayed for that precious sister of mine. Then one day when Robert and I were visiting Pam, she began to question, "Who is Jesus Christ? Why did He die? What difference does it make? What does it mean to me?"

I had told her all those things many times before, but she wasn't ready to listen. When we returned home, I mailed her a Bible and put her in touch with a Friendship Bible Coffee in her neighborhood. She went to her first Bible study, came home, sat on the sofa, prayed "the prayer of salvation," and trusted Christ as her Savior. Can you guess what she said to me? "Roberta, why didn't you tell me all this before?"

What makes patience and perseverance possible? Hope. Listen to what a secular fishing book has to say about the hope of fishermen. Consider this in the light of fishing for souls, and the meaning deepens.

> Fishing is hope experienced. When it comes to the human spirit, hope is all. Without hope, there is no yearning, no desire for a better tomorrow, and no belief that the next cast will bring the big strike.

> Fishermen are an optimistic lot, chronically optimistic, and to be optimistic in a slow bite is to thrive on hope alone. When asked, "How can you fish all day without a hit?" the true fisherman replies, "Hold it! I think I felt something." When the line again goes slack, he says, "He'll be back!" This is *hope defined*. Catching a fish is *hope affirmed*. A line in the water is *hope extended*.

> Fishermen fish hard. They fish long. They never stop casting, They fish from dawn 'til dusk, and into the night. They fish as if every cast will draw a strike. They troll on hour after hour without a hit. Without hope, they would quit—perhaps forever.

> Despite all the bad news, the threats to our waters and fishes, and to the places we so love and need, we

fishermen have a bright future. We have come a long way. We have gotten smarter, a little bolder in our views and actions, and we have a deeper grasp of the things that matter in the great web of life. We are learning to honor the fish we love. Never an idler's occupation, catching fish has historically been a matter of life and death. Successful fishermen are motivated, powerfully motivated, by something more than just catching fish.[1]

Now I ask you, when Jesus called us "fishers of men," don't you imagine He knew everything there was to know about fish, water, bait, and fishermen? Isn't the analogy wonderful? He gave us a mental image of a task He would equip us for. Fishers, not hunters. Hunters ambush. Fishers, not trackers. Trackers stalk. Fishers are patient, they persevere, they are motivated, and they thrive on hope. We are to be likewise.

LESSON NUMBER FOUR: We must fill our hearts with hope as we strive to be patient and to persevere with nonbelievers.

## How to Turn a Perfectly Normal Person into a Fisherman

Jesus said, "Follow Me, and I will make you fishers of men." He called for the disciples to *follow* Him. First of all that suggests that He would lead them, not drive or force them. Jesus was a loving, caring, and compassionate Master, Ruler, Leader, Commander, and world-class Fisherman. To follow Him meant trust, loyalty, and commitment to the Master. Jesus summoned "fishers of men" to the work of gathering people out of the sea of sin and death.

Jesus also looked for *teachable* followers. These first fishermen were unschooled, unsophisticated, and unknown. Well at least this unlikely crew of men didn't have to unlearn anything! Would you have started a worldwide ministry designed to transform humankind with this bunch? Hardly. But Jesus knew they had teachable hearts. They were fishermen, and fishing is an art and a science that requires discipline, skills, and a sincere desire to fish. The first "fishermen" were such men.

Jesus chose *available* followers. We read in Mark 1:18 that "at once they left their nets and followed him." Jesus still chooses those who are available. He doesn't seem to call idle people, but rather busy, productive individuals. Jesus made the overture first. They in turn made a conscious decision to become His disciples and followed him.

A careful study of Scripture indicates, however, that the disciples returned to their fishing in Galilee several times before the Lord actually appointed them to apostleship. They were not "microwave spiritual giants" (ready to serve in just minutes). It took time to grow in faith, just as it does today.

Sometimes it takes a few calls by God for the message to finally sink its hooks into us. We can relax in the knowledge that we are very much like those first fishermen. And we can expect that just as Jesus didn't give up on them, He has no intention of giving up on us. I love it when Jesus says, "I will make you fishers of men" because that means the full responsibility doesn't rest on our shoulders. He will make something out of us that we never thought possible. He will teach us the art of fishing for souls for His name's sake. He will empower us. He will prepare the hearts and minds of those we are yet to meet. And He will be there with us when we seize the moment. We need only to trust Him.

That we can do!

## HOOKS TO HANG YOUR HAT ON

- Jesus chooses followers who are available.
  How available are you?

- Get into the water this week where receptive, hungry nonbelievers live.

- Become a student of the nonbelievers God brings into your path. Spend 80 percent of the time listening to them and 20 percent sharing.

- The essence of the gospel is Christ died for our sins, He was buried, He was raised on the third day, and He was seen by many.

- Tell nonbelievers what they need to do with the gospel—trust Christ.

- Write out your three-minute testimony.

- Make a date for lunch, coffee, etc., with one of your party of three.
  Try to determine where your "three most wanted" are in their spiritual journeys and what their felt needs are.

## ALL THINGS CONSIDERED

1. Why do you personally want to share Christ with nonbelievers?

2. What felt need was met when you trusted Christ as Lord and Savior?

3. How can Jesus meet the felt needs in each of your party of three?

4. How would you describe "fishers of men"?

5. Jesus said, "Come, follow Me." Explain specifically what that means in your life.

6. What is the difference between being a believer "in" the world and being "of" it? Give an example.

7. Share the gospel in four main points. What does the nonbeliever need to do with this information?

8. "Always be prepared to give an answer to everyone who asks you to give the reason for the hope that you have. But do this with gentleness and respect" (1 Peter 3:15). Explain what is the hope you have and the reason for it.

9. How can we do this with "gentleness and respect" if the person is involved in a very sinful lifestyle and is unlovely, unashamed, uncharitable, and underhanded?

10. Share your three-minute testimony with a Christian friend or with your small group Bible study. Have them time it. It's work, but it will be worth it.

# CHAPTER FOUR

# SOW AND TELL

*"A farmer went out to sow his seed. . . .the word of God."*

LUKE 8:5, 11

hoa! Did you feel that one?" exclaimed my terror-stricken seatmate. "You know I fly a great deal," he said, squeezing a few words through his tightly clenched jaw, "but I've never been in such violent turbulence before. This is a real white-knuckle, heart-stopping, shirt-soaking kind of ride!"

"You know it's times like these when people make big promises to God," I replied.

He smiled nervously and nodded. I strongly suspected he had just finished his list of promises as I glanced at his colorless knuckles glued to the arm rests.

As we were plunging and vaulting all over the sky, we were well on our way to the Olympic gold in airplane gymnastics. Actually I marveled at the stress the aircraft was taking while I, of course, silently prayed for deliverance. These are the times you wish you had listened to the flight attendant's emergency instructions more carefully. But then what would I do with a life preserver over the Mojave Desert anyway?

I asked the frightened traveler, "What kind of promises do you think people make to God in a circumstance such as this?" I mentally congratulated myself, "What a great opener."

He thought a minute and then responded, "Well, I think people vow to clean up their lives, never tell another lie, never cheat on their expense account or mate again, go back to church, mend a broken relationship, be a better parent, spouse, or friend. You know, that sort of thing."

"Yes, I think you're right," I agreed. "People often make surprising promises to God when they think they're going down for the last time. But you know God made some pretty amazing promises to us." (Nonbelievers are usually curious to learn that God has made promises to people, especially ones of love rather than condemnation.) "Promises like God loves us so much and is so committed to us that there isn't anything we could do to make Him stop loving us."

"Nah, really?"

"Really. The Bible says God not only will forgive sinners who trust Him, but He remembers their sin no longer."

My seatmate replied, "Come on, you mean God has a bad memory? He isn't going to say, 'Oh it's you again. I see you're still up to your same old tricks'?"

"I know it's hard to believe," I said, "but the Bible says God has chosen to remember their sins no longer. If we seek Him, He promises us joy in a joyless world, peace in the midst of turmoil, and unconditional love."

"If only that were true," he responded, "but it's impossible for me to believe all that. I'm afraid I've been disappointed by too many promises from too many people to put my faith in someone I can't even see."

"Let me leave you with this thought," I answered. "The Lord is a promise-keeping God. He said that those who seek Him with all their hearts will find Him. Challenge Him with that promise."

My seatmate was quiet and reflective for quite some time after that. I didn't give him the whole gospel from sin to salvation. I just planted a seed and left the rest to the Holy Spirit.

## Sowers of the Gospel Spread It Freely

Jesus taught a parable (an earthly story with a spiritual message) about a farmer sowing his seed (Mark 4:3–20). The sower represents all those who share the gospel of Jesus Christ. The seed is the Word of God. Now the sower broadcasts the seed by hand, spreading it freely and widely. I find it interesting that the farmer does not limit his sowing to fertile soil.

Jesus said, "Go into all the world and preach the good news to all creation" (Mark 16:15). All the world? All creation? Sounds pretty universal to me. But wouldn't it be a waste of time and energy to sow seed on stony or thorny ground, or where birds will come along and devour it? That's where the Holy Spirit comes in. We are to spread the gospel to the four corners of the earth, but the responsibility for the results does not fall on us. It falls on the Holy Spirit. We disperse the seed; the soil determines the conditions; God dispenses the grace.

Perhaps right now you have some ground around you that

you've never considered "good soil." How about taking another look?

## Turn Curses into Blessings

Some people only speak the name of Jesus when they swear. Have you ever thought of this as a seed-sowing opportunity in weed-infested ground? Instead of getting angry or nervous when someone profanes the name of the Lord, consider answering with one of the following: "Do you know anything personally about the One you just called on?" "You must know Jesus very well; you use His name a lot." "Jesus is actually a pretty amazing person." "That's my best friend you're talking about."

But then get ready when they ask, "Tell me, what's amazing about this so-called best friend of yours?" What an opportunity to dig out some weeds of error and plant the truth. You see, many believe Jesus was just a good man, certainly not a personal God. Tell them about your best friend, just as the staff from the Southwestern Women's Conference did as an exercise at a staff retreat. This is how they described their best friend:

"I'd like you to meet my friend Jesus. He is my best friend and companion. He's the only friend I'll ever need. Even when I'm not always there for Him, He's always there for me. If you ever need to know something, just ask Him. He is so full of wisdom. He is always eager to hear from me. In all the years I've known Him, He has never failed me. He even saved my life! He has rescued me from trouble time and time again. He has comforted me in my grief. He's as close as the mention of His name. He's been a wonderful counselor for me, and I know He can do the same for you. He's an author of the number one bestseller of all time. He has an incredible imagination.

"You wouldn't believe the things He's created! He is commander in chief of a great army. He is very prestigious and knows just everybody. He loves me unconditionally. He's the only person I know that died and rose again. He is very wealthy and owns many mansions and is preparing one for me. Once you meet Him, you just can't forget Him. He'd really like to get to know you better. Would you like me to introduce you to Him?"

The list could go on and on. Make a list of your own and personalize it. You'll find it's really quite easy to tell others about Jesus being your best friend. And a seed of blessing can be planted where curses were found before.

## Sowing in Unlikely Soil

Obviously not all ground looks fertile, but we are to sow the seeds in spite of how unfit we may assess the condition of the soil to be. Good earth may lie just below the surface. Ask Kurt Salierno.

"Anybody got a drink?" asked Max as he made the rounds of his derelict friends one freezing night. Max was once employed and had a family, but he had lost his job, felt helpless, started drinking, and ended up living on Burnside Street, which is the center of skid row in Portland, Oregon. During the winter alcohol served as antifreeze, among other things, for these street people, helping them survive the night. Groups of destitute and miserable people would huddle together, piling on top of one another to stay warm. Many would even sleep in Dumpsters buried under garbage to take the chill off. Burnside was an unlikely place to find "good soil." Most of us probably would not have bothered testing this soil.

But Kurt Salierno felt a calling from God to live among these street people who called him " preacher boy." He wanted to love them to Jesus. For two and half years he ministered to drunks, prostitutes, bums, and social deviates. People without Christ. People without hope.

One night an ice storm was especially brutal to those whose homes were the filth-filled Dumpsters, concrete pavements, and dangerous alleys. Kurt huddled together with the other street people to try to make it through the night. Since Kurt was literally breathing down Max's neck, he thought he'd drum up a conversation. He asked, "Max, have you ever thought about getting off the streets?" "No," he said. "The street is my home. I won't ever leave this place." Kurt questioned further. "Are you happy here?" Max replied, "Oh I don't know. I'm surviving just like you." Kurt then told Max about the joy in his heart despite these present conditions. He told him about the One who loved him enough to die for him. That really got Max's attention. "What are you talking about?" asked Max. That was the question Kurt was waiting for, so he unfolded the greatest story ever told. Max heard how Jesus died for him on the cross because He loved him so much.

It was hard for Max to believe in such love. His kids used to love him but not anymore. His wife used to love him but didn't want him now. "Max, you are loved by Jesus," Kurt repeated many times over the next days. Max needed to hear this; he wanted to hear it. Jesus met him at his point of need—to be loved. Before the week was out, Max asked, "Is it too late for me to have that eternal life and joy?" That remarkable night Max prayed and gave his life to Jesus.

Amid the cheap wine, smelly bodies, urine, and vomit, Jesus Christ broke through. The one truth that was especially meaningful to Max was that Christ wants us to love others, just as He loves us. Those were words he intended to live by, and he repeated them over and over again.

A few days later another major storm developed. About eight street people huddled together as close as they could, trying to live through another freezing night. Somebody had to be on top of the heap and be most exposed to the cold. Max choose the top because "Christ wants us to love others, just as He loves us." As soon as the rain hit him, it froze. It was a long and bitterly cold night.

"I can't feel my feet," exclaimed a strangely smiling Max in the morning. His shoes were covered with ice, he wore no socks, and his feet were almost completely white, but he was content to have been a true servant that night. Max eventually had to have his legs amputated from his knees down because of gangrene. Despite the amputations, the gangrene spread and not long after took his life. But even in the hospital many commented, "There was something different about Max. He was so full of joy and kept talking about Jesus."

Questionable soil? God knew the "good earth." And Kurt planted a seed many of us might never have planted.[1]

## *Gardeners Study the Nature of the Soil*

Any gardener understands you need to study the nature of the soil in order to receive the best results from what you plant. You prepare the soil differently depending on whether it is fertile or sandy, stony or thorny, alkaline or acidic.

Remember the personality types we discussed in chapter two? We need to prepare the "soil" a bit differently with each of these individuals. To meet them where they are. To seek to understand the best way to relate to them.

For example, the gospel should be presented logically to melancholies. They love organization. *The Four Spiritual Laws* booklet by Bill Bright or *The Search* booklet by Search Ministries can be great evangelistic tools to use with them.

Melancholy people are cautious and usually need time to think things over. Be patient with them. When they trust their lives to Jesus, they discover He is a God of order, not chaos, as He plans their lives carefully. "'For I know the plans I have for you,' declares the Lord, 'plans to prosper you and not to harm you, plans to give you hope and a future'" (Jeremiah 29:11).

Cholerics understand obedience and authority. Remember, they're the "Confess, repent, and believe, or you're going to hell" kind of people. Net it out for them. It's best not to "dance around" cholerics. Since cholerics are goal oriented, they understand heavenly rewards. "I the Lord search the heart and examine the mind, to reward a man according to his conduct, according to what his deeds deserve" (Jeremiah 17:10). And they know all about wages. "For the wages of sin is death, but the gift of God is eternal life" (Romans 6:23). A choleric is so used to running things himself he will often have difficulty giving control of his life to the Lord. But as he does, his understanding of obedience to God is firmly implanted. He is awed by the Almighty.

Give sanguines plenty of attention. Allow them to express themselves; they'll insist on doing it anyway! Most sanguines have endearing, childlike ways and are trusting, receptive, and open. They usually relate to these words of Jesus: "I tell you the truth, anyone who will not receive the kingdom of God like a little child will never enter it" (Mark 10:15). Rules, laws, and regulations in Christianity are often what nonbelieving sanguines fear. They're scared to death someone will tell them to sit up, put up, and button up! They need to hear the gospel for what it is—love. "For God so loved the world" (John 3:16). Sanguines then will often love the Lord deeply and unabashedly.

Be sure to convey the message of peace to phlegmatics. They are nonaggressive, rather nonemotional individuals. It's best not to press them too hard. They need lots of space. They love to hear how Jesus is the Prince of Peace who has given them peace with the Father. A promise that may especially minister to them is "Peace I leave with you; my peace I give you. I do not give to you as the world gives. Do not let your hearts be troubled and do not be afraid" (John 14:27). They usually grow to love the Lord in a low-key, soft-spoken, collected manner.

These principles are not hard and fast rules, but they certainly have helped me understand the personality traits of nonbelievers so I could communicate better with them. Jesus always met people where they were emotionally, physically, and spiritually. The more informed we are about our nonbelieving friends, the better able we are to meet them at their points of need.

One note of caution. We cannot always accurately determine the soil condition. Only God knows the heart. But we can always be available to sow His message in the best way we know how.

## *It's Always Planting Season*

"Did your friend rise again?" asked Terri. This is hardly a casual question. I don't imagine we'd put it on the same level as "So how's the family?" or "Paper or plastic?" But my dear friend Terri Politan scattered some seeds in a most creative way when she was having lunch one afternoon. As she walked up to the cash register to pay, she noticed on the wall a portrait of a man with a turban on his head and a halo over him. Thinking he was probably a guru of some kind, she said to the owner, "May I ask, who is this man?"

"Ah," the man exclaimed. "He is the one who looks after me. I pray to him, and he helps me with all my needs. He looks after this place, and he even looks after you to see that you have good service and food."

Terri is a tender-hearted, godly woman with a gracious and quiet spirit. If she ever insulted you (which she wouldn't), you would find yourself thanking her for her deep insight. So Terri casually and courteously asked, "Where does he live?"

The owner answered, "Oh, he's dead, but his spirit lives."

Then Terri asked the most creative and critical question: "Did he rise again?"

"Well, no he didn't," replied the man.

Terri then pulled out a seed of truth and gave it to the man, saying, "I have a Savior, whose name is Jesus Christ. I pray to Him, and He cares for me and all my needs. He rose again from the dead because the grave could not hold Him. He is a living God." The man listened, and a seed was gently planted.

This was a short, easy conversation any of us could have initiated. The man was quite willing and unashamed to tell of the dead person in whom he depended. Should we not be eager to speak of our living Savior who will never leave us or forsake us? Seed-sowing opportunities abound, but we must be watchful or we'll easily miss them.

One day, several years ago, I had just given a lecture at our Community Bible Study that included John 3:16: "For God so loved the world that he gave his one and only Son, that whoever believes in him shall not perish but have eternal life." What a wonderful verse. "Eternal life"—what a hope. "His one and only Son"—what a gift. "Whoever believes in him"—what an opportunity. "Shall not perish"—what a certainty. Thinking on these words I happily dashed into the grocery store to get a few things for dinner. I was humming to myself somewhere between the red peppers, yellow squash, and zucchini when a young stock clerk approached me and asked, "What could you possibly be so happy about?"

I thought, "He approached me. He asked me. So I'm going to tell him." I simply said, "Jesus loves me and I love Him! That's why I'm happy."

He said, "I knew it had to be something really big and important."

And to this inquiring teenager, I replied, "You got that right!"

A simple answer to a simple question. But it is an age-old question that many are asking today. "How can you be happy in such a miserable world filled with hate, war, drugs, abuse, greed, sickness, and violence?" Answer? "Jesus Christ." Sometimes that's all the answer we can give them at the moment. But He's been the perfect answer for two thousand years. Today is no different. I may never see this young man again, but a seed was definitely planted.

It was so easy. However, acting on such opportunities does take just a bit of boldness and courage. We're afraid people will think we're weird religious fanatics, out of touch with reality. But we must not forget that so many people are hungry for answers in this chaotic and complicated society. We know the answer, and all we may be called upon to do is plant the seed: "Jesus Christ is the answer." Allow the Holy Spirit to do His perfect work. Let Him worry about the results.

## The Art of Planting Seedlings

Just as we must be open to every opportunity, we need to know what to do with them when they come.

A distraught young woman showed up at a friend's front door one afternoon. She was having marital problems and was considering hiring an attorney, and she simply needed to talk. Since she was a nonbeliever, my friend felt this presented a perfect opportunity to share the gospel with her. Hearts are often more open during times of suffering.

"I think maybe I said too much," my friend later explained to me. "I wanted to witness to Judy so I told her, well, I guess everything I knew."

"You didn't go through the whole account of lamb sacrifices, blood atonements, and the temple destruction in A.D. 70, did you? You didn't give her a minicourse in Genesis to Revelation, did you?"

"Well you were the one I first heard it from!" she replied.

"Yes," I said, "but you were so hungry to hear more and more. You were intent on finding some answers. You questioned continually. Was Judy asking questions? Did you sense she was really thirsty for God?"

My friend replied, "No, I guess she really wasn't. But I wanted her to know why Jesus was the answer to her problems. I thought if I could only tell her one more thing, one more verse, one more promise of God, then she would truly understand."

"What did she say when you were finished?" I asked.

"Well, Judy leaned way over toward me with a very penetrating expression and said in a low voice, 'So now, do you think I should see an attorney or what?' That's when I knew she probably wasn't listening!"

When we dump our reservoir of biblical knowledge on the fragile nonbeliever, out comes Adam and Eve, Abraham and Moses, David and Solomon, the ark of the covenant, the sacrifices, the prophets, the law, and a detailed description of the final week of Christ's life on earth. We've just unloaded enough root stimulator to overwhelm our seedling. A good rule of thumb: don't answer questions they're not asking. You'll be kept busy enough just answering the ones they are asking. Effective communication of the gospel is not how much you talk but how much is received.

## *Satisfy Their Thirst*

How do we keep from drowning our "seedling" in a sea of doctrine? The answer is really quite easy. Become totally familiar with basic gospel facts. Jesus gave a simple, clear message that is easy to understand and receive for those who are truly seeking after God. Here's one way to present the gospel in three main points.

### GOD'S POSITION

What does God say about our human condition?

1. Everyone has sinned: "For all have sinned and fall short of the glory of God" (Romans 3:23).
2. Our sins separate us from God: "But your iniquities have separated you from your God; your sins have hidden his face from you, so that he will not hear" (Isaiah 59:2).
3. Everyone who sins is subject to die: "For the wages of sin is death, but the free gift of God is eternal life in Christ Jesus our Lord" (Romans 6:23, NASB).

### GOD'S PLAN

What is God's provision for our dilemma?

1. He saves us from our sins: "For Christ died for sins once for all, the righteous for the unrighteous, to bring you to God" (1 Peter 3:18).
2. He gives us eternal life: "For God so loved the world that he gave his one and only Son, that whoever believes in him shall not perish but have eternal life" (John 3:16).

OUR DECISION

Our choice is either to receive or reject Jesus.

1. In order to receive Jesus, we must confess our sins and He will forgive us: "If we confess our sins, he is faithful and just and will forgive us our sins and purify us from all unrighteousness" (1 John 1:9).
2. If we believe that Jesus is Lord, we will be saved: "If you confess with your mouth, 'Jesus is Lord,' and believe in your heart that God raised him from the dead, you will be saved" (Romans 10:9).

As people grow in their understanding, they will be ready for a deeper and more comprehensive study of God's Word, but in the beginning we need to learn to communicate the basic message of the gospel without overwhelming them with information. Then perhaps one wonderful day this person will stand face to face, heart to heart before God, perfect in Him. And guess what? God will turn and say to you, "Well done, my good and faithful servant."

## Nourishment for the Seedling

A little seedling would wither and die if its roots didn't start digging down into the earth. How would it survive when the storms came and the winds blew if its roots remained on the surface? It needs stability. In a similar way, the new believer needs to be rooted and grounded in the Word of God so he will hold firm when the storms of life blow.

Are we there to help then also? Do we provide opportunities for growth in Bible studies? Are we informed about the Bible studies in our church, town, or neighborhood? Perhaps we would be willing to meet one-on-one to investigate the claims of Jesus Christ, to study the Gospel of John, or to study the names of Christ. When people first hear the gospel, they need to learn how to investigate the truth, how to study the Word. This is where the "nourisher" comes in to foster development and promote growth. Maybe that's us. Perhaps someone else has already planted the seed and now our job is to provide the water and fertilizer.

It is really quite simple. Just ask your friend or your party of three, "Would you consider meeting with me one day a week for six weeks to study the claims of Jesus Christ in the Gospel of John?" Does that scare the liver right out of you? Then perhaps you have several friends who would join you. It's a challenging study even for an "old" believer.

I suggest first doing such a study on your own. (Your Christian bookstore will help you find good resource materials.) Then study with nonbelievers, new believers, and mature believers all together—ideally at least one of each. The study will bless them all, for no one in all of history is more wise, loving, graceful, radical, exciting, compassionate, powerful, and merciful than our all-sufficient Savior. Discover Him anew with greater depth. Study the amazing claims of Jesus Christ, provide nourishment for the new believer or the seeker, and be blessed.

If that seems more that we can do, we can at least give that nonbeliever a book or a tape. We need to find a couple of books that tell nonbelievers everything we would like to but maybe don't have the time, the words, or the boldness. Let me suggest a few to get you started.

*More than a Carpenter* by Josh McDowell is for people who are skeptical about Jesus' deity, His resurrection, and His ability to change lives.

*Mere Christianity* by C. S. Lewis is definitely for the intellectual skeptic who believes people must check their brains at the door in order to trust Christ. C. S. Lewis was an Oxford scholar and atheist who set about to discredit the Bible and in the process trusted his life to Jesus.

*Classic Christianity* by Bob George explains the difference between being religious and being a Christian. It's a good study for a person who thinks religion is all dos, don'ts, and works.

*Born Again* by Chuck Colson was the first "Christian book" my husband ever read. Between the pages Robert met Jesus. As he read the story about Watergate, he saw a man, Chuck Colson, to whom he could relate: hard driving, aggressive, and strong-willed. He concluded if God could forgive Colson for all that he had done and been, then God would forgive him. This book, which speaks powerfully to strong men and women, was one of the vehicles God used to bring my husband to Christ.

*A Shepherd Looks at Psalm 23* by Phillip Keller is a tender, sensitive book that simply speaks to the heart about the Good Shepherd and how He cares for His sheep. It's a wonderful book to draw someone closer to investigating our Savior.

## Transplanting from Pots

The time will come when our seedlings have outgrown their pots. When their roots are strong, they will need to move on to grow to their fullest potential.

They may move out of our lives to distant places, decide to attend another church, or begin a Bible study of their own. We must trust the God who brought them to us in the first place to continue the seeding, cultivating, watering, and propagating into other gardens. When the time comes for reaping, He will harvest. "Being confident of this, that he who began a good work in you will carry it on to completion until the day of Christ Jesus" (Philippians 1:6).

### HOOKS TO HANG YOUR HAT ON

- Pray to be aware of seed-sowing opportunities.
- Give people enough to enable them to grow, but don't drown them with more than they can absorb at a time.
- Broadcast your seeds to "all creation."
- Study the soil type before sowing.
- Tell your party of three about your best friend, Jesus.
- Don't answer questions they're not asking.
- Provide opportunities for growth in Bible studies.
- Share well-chosen books with your seeker friends.
- Trust God with their ultimate, long-term growth. He will complete the work He began.

## ALL THINGS CONSIDERED

1. Share a time when you have planted the seed of the Word of God. Did you use books, tapes, concerts, a word, a verse, a truth, a unique situation? What was the result?

2. Do you ever feel that a person's relationship to God is such a personal matter that you might be interfering? What would Jesus do in such a situation?

3. Have you ever failed to witness to people because they already had a form of religion? How can we present the gospel without attacking them or their belief system? Who does the convicting of sin and truth?

4. Does the Word of God stand on its own or does it need to be defended? Does Scripture stand in judgment of humankind or does humankind stand in judgment of the Scriptures? How does our understanding of these answers help us in witnessing?

5. Review three main points of the gospel message: God's position, God's plan, and our decision. Write out the Scripture verses. Memorize them. Stick to the main message.

6. What if nonbelievers ask how we feel about reincarnation, abortion, or the long lost tribe of a country that has never heard of Jesus? How should we handle such questions?

7. How can we keep from drowning our seedling in a sea of theology?

8. How can we discern if someone is a seeker of God, not really interested, or just argumentative? Discuss some methods of dealing with the uninterested or the argumentative so as not to offend them.

9. Write a letter to an imaginary friend or your party of three, telling them about your best friend, Jesus. Tell them how you met Him, who He is, what He's done, what He means to you, promises He's made, how He changed your life. It's a non-threatening way of witnessing.

10. "Be self-controlled and alert. Your enemy the devil prowls around like a roaring lion looking for someone to devour" (1 Peter 5:8). What sort of things might Satan do to confuse the nonbeliever as you share the gospel? How does a believer who is "self-controlled and alert" act? Notice the verse says the devil is like a roaring lion; it doesn't say he is one.

# CHAPTER FIVE

# THE TRUE LIFE OF THE PARTY

*Christ companied with sinners without becoming complicated with their sins.*

HOWARD HENDRICKS

I t was the grandest church in town sitting in a place of prominence high on a hill. All agreed it was a work of art and a thing of beauty. The people attending were fine, lovely, caring people. Well, at least they seemed to care for one another, but it was a rather exclusionary congregation. They would always smile and nod to the poor, the thirsty, the wounded, the spiritually needy, and the desperately lost. But few ever invited them into their household of faith to celebrate, to worship, to party, to sing, to share, to be loved. The lost remained lost and watched daily as the big wooden doors would open wide only to close them out.

We believers in Jesus Christ are the household of God's people, the church. Have we flung open the doors of our homes, hearts, and churches to the lost? Are we truly willing to receive, to invite, to extend hospitality to those not of the household of faith? It's often difficult, isn't it? Sometimes the lost speak coarsely, have divergent views, are unlovely, and are not easy to accept into our hearts. Sometimes we think of them as "untouchables." Besides, it's just so comfortable to be around Christians all the time, so affirming and encouraging. They speak our special language and know the verses we memorize, the songs we sing, the struggles we have, and the Lord we love.

Although believers must continue to meet together and be strengthened, God did not call us to live in our "holy huddles" in a spiritual quarantine. We are to reach out to the lost and invite them to the social gatherings, the songfests, and the celebrations of our lives. May the Lord use this book to awaken us to witness and celebrate the Living Christ with those outside the circle of faith. For indeed, is He not the "true life of the party"?

## Tax Collector's Party

In the first century being a tax collector was like having a license for extortion. Tax collectors had the key to the bank. They could send out tax bills for whatever Rome wanted and could tack on whatever they wanted—10 percent, 20 percent, 30 percent, or more—to pocket in their jeans. If people didn't pay, tax collectors could encourage a few Roman soldiers to visit them some dark night. It's not surprising that tax collectors were considered sleazy, greedy, deceitful characters.

Matthew, one of Jesus' disciples, was a hated tax collector. When Matthew became a follower of Jesus Christ, it cost him a small fortune to leave the fraternity of tax collectors behind. The disciples who were fishermen also left their profession, but they could return to their boats and fishing nets if they chose. Matthew could never go back once he left.

Even though Matthew was just a rookie at following Christ, he did not follow Him in secret. Instead he decided to throw a big dinner party, announcing to all of his tax collecting buddies that he was closing up shop in the extortion business. He was signing up for a tour of duty with Jesus of Nazareth, and he wanted them to meet Him (Luke 5:27–32).

A great banquet was held in Jesus' honor. Never one to let an opportunity pass Him by, Jesus willingly associated with lost souls. And there was certainly a houseful at Matthew's that night. Matthew had provided an opportunity for his buddies to be influenced by Jesus and His disciples. This could have been the first friendship evangelistic dinner!

Matthew risked bringing together this unlikely combination of people in the hopes that something significant would take place. Maybe he thought it was a long shot, but he was willing to host it and to fund it. However, the Pharisees and the teachers of the law had a serious problem with Matthew's guest list: Jesus and His followers were rubbing shoulders with tax collectors and sinners at this party. The Pharisees considered these people irreligious riffraff. "Holy people" simply didn't spend time with the likes of these for they were profane, sinful, greedy, immoral people. Better to write them off than soil one's reputation. As the religious elite of the day, the Pharisees were so obsessed with impressing others with their own self-righteousness that their hearts had become cold to lost people. They prided themselves in obeying all of the laws, but their hearts were far from God.

Upon hearing of the Pharisees' displeasure at the guest list, Jesus said (and I paraphrase), "Healthy people don't need a doctor; sick people do. My heart's desire is for you to show mercy, a forgiving spirit, not just strict adherence to rules and regulations, not just sacrifice. I have come to call sinners to repentance." Jesus always made time for sinners. Lost, irreligious people who are on a fast track to destruction matter to God. Lost people should matter to us too.

### Let's Throw a Matthew Evangelistic Party

Sometimes as believers we too are on the "spiritual giant, perfectionist track." We may gauge our spiritual maturity by the number of verses we can quote, how much we serve at church, how many seminars we attend, how many tapes we listen to and Christian books we read. We might even look a little Pharisaic by completely separating ourselves from nonbelievers.

How can we be more like Jesus in relating to nonbelievers? Have you ever considered throwing a Matthew-style, evangelistic dinner party? Over the years a number of our friends have done this on a regular basis. Before they ever invited even one person, they would pray about their "irreligious guest list." At least one other Christian couple was always invited. They first started with a few neighbors, then friends, coworkers, golfing buddies, tennis partners, and even strangers they met on airplanes. (One traveling sales rep claims he gets to know his seatmates on coast-to-coast flights far better than he knows his next-door neighbors.)

They planned everything from backyard barbecues to sit-down dinners to lakeside picnics. The focus of the get-together was to develop a relationship with the unsaved. If God provided any openings for the Christians to share their faith, then they did so without hesitation. Of course the Christians looked for opportunities, and the Lord honored their efforts. Much prayer always preceded these affairs, and lives were transformed over picnic benches, charcoal burgers, and dining room tables.

One couple planned several ski weekend parties at their condo every year for the sole purpose of friendship evangelism. "Over the past five years," the husband said, "we've had more fun than I thought possible, made more good friends than we deserve, and have led more than thirty or forty people to the Lord."

## Breaking the Ice

Whatever the nature of the get-together, before you eat, be sure someone prays a blessing over your meal, thanking the Lord also for those new friends around your table. Then we like to start right in with some ice breakers to get to know everyone at the table.

One evening at dinner I talked about the movie *Dances with Wolves* and how the native Americans were given names that described their personalities—"Wind in His Hair," "Kicking Bird," and of course "Dances with Wolves." So we went around the table and gave ourselves and sometimes each other descriptive names. It was great fun. Our daughter, Shannon, won the title "Standing with Fists." A major league baseball player who was with us that evening earned the name "Standing with Bat." I became "Happy Bird," and Robert was "Love Chunks." (Trust me, it was a term of endearment.) We had "Lonely Dove," "Peaceful Bird," "Busy Beaver" and all sorts of interesting names.

Although this doesn't sound terribly spiritual, it can reveal something about the person we might not otherwise know. It also can open up conversation on a deeper level. For example, what is the "beaver" so busy doing? Is it satisfying? What else would he or she rather be doing? Is busyness contentment? Why do you call yourself "lonely"? How do you define "lonely"? All of these can become good material for conversation.

Think about some questions you could ask a guest. Around Christmas time, Thanksgiving, or Easter you can ask guests to share their best memory of that holiday. What family tradition was meaningful to them as children? You will be amazed how such questions bring out spiritual conversation. Listen carefully as someone shares a special memory from a holiday. Does it include any spiritual experience or religious tradition? If so, you might ask, "How did that experience contribute to your understanding of the holiday? Do you still celebrate in a similar way?" Then you might share how you celebrate from a spiritual point of view at home, at church, and with friends.

Another ice breaker is "If you could be anyone in the world, who would you be?" Suppose someone says he would like to be a powerful ruler and decree peace to every country and person. You might ask how he envisions peace. Is it just absence of war? Or is there more to peace? That could open a great discussion on the Prince of Peace—who He was, what kind of peace He brought, and how we can have His peace.

Or ask, "If you could do anything in the world, what would you do? Why?" If someone says she would like to be rich, you could ask what she would do with all her money. Discuss the power of money to buy material things and the powerlessness of money to purchase such things as true love, wisdom, inner peace, inner beauty, a good marriage, a guilt-free conscience, and contentment. Share the things in your life that money is powerless to buy. A guilt-free conscience is a great point to discuss. If appropriate, you could tell them how Jesus took the sin and guilt of your personal past upon Himself.

Ask them to share the best day of their lives and why. If they could have made it any better, what would they have added? Talk about what makes a day the "best." Share one of the best days of your life. I usually mention a great memory in my life such as the birth of a child, the day Robert and I renewed our wedding vows, a dream fulfilled in one of my children. Then sometimes I add the day I trusted Christ, why it was the best, and why life is better as a result.

However, we need to be cautious and sensitive about directing conversation into a spiritual dimension. We don't want guests to feel as if this was a staged event. If these topics of conversation open up possibilities for spiritual discussion, wonderful. If not, we are still developing friendships and extending hospitality.

Did it ever occur to you how much Jesus loved dinner parties? Check out all the times in the Bible that He attended them. He was no dull, tedious, wearisome, fuddy-duddy of a guest. He was and is the most outrageously joyful and delightful dinner guest you could ever invite into your home. He brightens the moment, challenges the mind, inspires the spirit, and rejoices the heart. Ask Jesus about friendship evangelism: "Lord, if You were me, what would You do in my little corner of the world?" And when He provides an answer, act on it. Extend the opportunity to others of inviting Him into their hearts.

Maybe you don't have a condo in Colorado, a houseboat on

the lake, or a dining room that seats more than four, but you do have a table, a testimony, and a Teacher who will empower you with all you need. You have an eternal future with Christ, a power within you, and a God who is crazy about you and your lost friends. Share Him in whatever circumstances God has given you. Share Him fully, freely, and faithfully.

## So What's Your Life Philosophy?

Not every opportunity for sharing Jesus will come through your own instigation. Natural opportunities abound in all sorts of social settings.

Acapulco Bay, a moonlight cruise, good food to eat, lots of champagne, and a boatload of sunburned nonbelievers. What an evangelistic opportunity! Be honest; I'll bet that's not what you were thinking.

Every year my husband's company would present its top salespeople and executives with the President's Club award, consisting of a trip to some wonderful destination, all expenses paid. This particular year we were in Mexico.

The alcohol was flowing like the wake behind us, the conversation was peppered with unsavory talk, and there I sat with my usual Perrier and lime—my idea of a mixed drink. One of the young salesmen who worked for my husband decided to make an impression on the boss's wife. And indeed he did.

"Mrs. Kuhne, may I sit here?" he asked.

"Please do." I replied.

"Look at this view!" he began. "Acapulco Bay in the middle of a miserable January winter in Chicago. What could be better? I worked hard to get here, and now I'm able to reap the rewards of my efforts. This is the best that life can offer. I've reached the pinnacle." (Remember he was young.) "What in life could be greater than success and the ability to enjoy it?"

Boy, did he sit next to the right person! Where should I begin? He had given me so much material in such a short span of time I salivated at the opportunity. "John, this certainly is one great spot. I'm sure glad not to be sitting in six feet of snow in Chicago. But you just made an interesting comment when you said you've reached the pinnacle of life. I'd be interested in hearing about your life philosophy."

I've discovered this is usually an excellent question to ask nonbelievers. It's nonthreatening and offers lots of openings for spiritual conversation. It's good small talk that has the potential for major life changes. Most people have never thought through their beliefs long enough to verbalize them clearly, but many will start right in to tell you anyway. I think John was developing his beliefs even as he recounted them to me.

He said, "Today when I went parasailing over Acapulco Bay, I felt a oneness with the earth, the sky, the sea, the birds of the air, and the fish of the sea. As I sat in the harness with the parachute above me, I felt so peaceful. It was kind of like a spiritual experience, a oneness with the universe. That's what I'm seeking in life—oneness and peace. That's my life philosophy."

"I went parasailing today too," I replied. "I experienced twenty minutes of sheer terror sprinkled with a few moments of absolute peace. Actually I loved it, but I didn't feel a oneness with the world. I'm particularly happy that I didn't feel a oneness with the sharks in the bay. Seriously though, you sound as if you're sincerely seeking peace. Tell me what you believe about God. Do you think peace can be found in God?"

As I asked for details, John was at a loss for what he really believed. "We have this understanding, God and I," he said. Then he painted a verbal picture of a god I couldn't imagine, and I'm not sure he could either.

So I asked him, "John, what is your source of truth for what you believe?" When he answered, "Shirley MacLaine," I knew this would be an interesting evening. If he was resting his eternal security on MacLaine's words, how did he know she was accurate? Some say it doesn't matter what you believe as long as you are sincere. But you can be sincerely wrong and end up eternally separated from God. Graciously ask them to defend their beliefs.

"John," I said, "if you believe you are God,"—he claimed he was—"who created the world? How are you able to be Creator and creature? Why don't you have peace all the time? If you are God, where will you spend eternity?" He really couldn't answer.

If we ask the right questions, it often reveals to people on what shaky ground they are resting their beliefs. Frequently they come to that conclusion on their own. Let nonbelievers talk their hearts out. Our job is to be available, listen carefully, and use probing questions, all the while praying for discernment and wisdom.

New Age philosophy abounds, seeping into many facets of education, the workplace, and even some churches. Perhaps you work with someone, have someone living in your home, or are friends with one who holds this belief system. I think you'll find the book *Out on a Broken Limb* by F. LaGard Smith to be most helpful. Smith, a Christian attorney, wrote it as a retort to MacLaine's book on her belief system. It's also an excellent book to recommend to New Agers. You might suggest that since they are students of spiritual things, they owe it to themselves to investigate the other side. Smith provides a firm biblical foundation on which to confront the New Age philosophy.

Ask permission to share what you believe about God and your source for truth. This will help them see the firm foundation on which Christianity is based. We have a truth source—the Scriptures, which stand the test of historical accuracy. Archaeological findings consistently prove the accuracy of the Scriptures. The Bible has hundreds of prophecies that Jesus Christ fulfilled. There are eyewitness accounts of His ministry, death, and resurrection. Most importantly the person of Jesus Christ has transformed millions of lives. Here's your three-minute testimony time: "He transformed my life. May I tell you how?"

### Be Prepared If They Ask for Proof

If in the process of explaining the basis for our own beliefs someone challenges us about the accuracy and authority of the Scriptures, we need to be prepared to respond. Knowing a few of the prophecies Jesus fulfilled can be a good place to begin. Here are some you might commit to memory:

Isaiah 7:14—Born of a virgin.
Isaiah 11:1, 10—A descendant of Jesse and thus in the Davidic line.
Micah 5:2—The Messiah would come from Bethlehem.
Isaiah 49:3—He would manifest God's glory.

Isaiah 49:7; 53:1, 3—He would be rejected by Israel.

Isaiah 49:7; 52:15—He would be worshiped by Gentiles.

Isaiah 53:4–6, 10–12—He would bear the sins of the world.

Isaiah 53—Speaks of the suffering and passion of Christ.

Psalm 22:1–21—He would be crucified.

Psalm 22:18—Soldiers would gamble for His clothing.

Psalm 34:20—His bones would not be broken.

Psalm 41:9—One close to Him would betray Him.

Psalm 68:18—He would ascend into heaven.

Psalm 69:21—He would be offered gall and vinegar for His thirst on the cross.

Psalm 96:13—He will return to judge the world.

It's amazing how often God opens up windows of opportunities. Ask the Lord to make you intently aware of these times. He's faithful. He will. Then allow the Holy Spirit to guide the conversation. He's gone ahead of us anyway and prepared the hearts. Don't be afraid to rub shoulders with irreligious people. Their frantic attempts at good times indicate a desperate search for real answers to life.

John will never know true peace until he experiences a oneness with Jesus Christ. And that's what I eventually told him. I pray he'll remember that when he comes to the end of himself one day.

### Unlikely People Reached by Unlikely People

When people come to the end of themselves, they are more willing to acknowledge that they are on a dead-end path. And perhaps the best person to show them the right path is someone who also came to the end of himself. Take Frank Macias's story of how God used "Billy Goat," the town drunk, to bring him to the Lord:

"Billy was once a hard-core alcoholic. When he got saved, he came after the one person in town he knew he could relate to—me! The guy was a pest. There's nothing worse than a reformed drunk who gets religion. He kept inviting me to come to church with him. He had to be kidding. I was too busy partying, drinking, selling and doing drugs.

"I used to go to the Indian reservations and take cases of alcohol to trade for peyote and mescaline. Since the age of eleven, I had been fighting, stealing, and partying. My life was a downward spiral from cigarettes and beer to marijuana, cocaine, and LSD. The problem was that the thrill had to get bigger and better. Sin will take you deeper than you ever thought you would go. It will keep you longer than you ever thought you would stay. It will grip you tighter than you ever thought it could hold.

"One night my wife Kathy and I were going to go out to a party, the kind of party that spelled trouble. About ten or twenty kegs of beer and five or ten pounds of marijuana was common. Billy Goat was after me again, so I told Kathy, 'Look, Honey, I want to get this guy off my back. So we'll go to his church party and then head for the real party.'

"When we walked into the church, everyone was sitting on the carpet, so we did too. The band played Christian music, and when the lead singer began to preach the gospel, my throat choked up, my eyes welled with tears, and I started to cry. I was so embarrassed; I couldn't understand what was happening to me. I heard that Jesus Christ died just for me on the cross so that I could be forgiven of all my sins. I'd never heard this before, and I was born in the United States! It was music to my ears and healing to my bones. He said I could go to heaven if I trusted Christ. Then he offered an invitation that if anyone wanted to make that decision he should step forward. I couldn't believe it! I jumped to my feet and went forward. I wept for at least an hour afterward. It was an awesome evening. I found forgiveness, and I made peace with my Maker, my God, and my Creator."

Today Frank Macias serves as chaplain of Durango Juvenile Detention Center in Arizona. All the kids call him Brother Frank. They can't tell him anything that surprises him. He's been there, he knows what they're thinking, he knows what they're up to. As a believer, Billy Goat wasn't afraid to rub shoulders with irreligious people; neither is Frank. He does it everyday and in the process tells them about Jesus. Frank also knows a good party when he sees one. It's the one in the church gym where everyone sits on the floor, drinks pop, and sings about Jesus!

Billy Goat was an unlikely person, Frank Macias was an unlikely person, and perhaps so were we before we trusted Christ. God just happens to use unlikely people. Our lives may never take us into Billy's or Frank's world, but everyday we meet irreligious people. When was the last time we rubbed shoulders with them? When was the last time we invited a nonbeliever to a church event, a Christian concert, a Christian wedding, the dedication of a new baby, the baptism of a believer, or a party that celebrates such an occasion? We never know where it might lead.

## We Need a Holy Boldness to Speak His Name

Crystal goblets were tinkling, soft music was playing, and the air was filled with philosophical conversation when a young party-goer announced, "I am in my last life, my last existence. I believe I have reached perfection."

"Well, well," said an older gentleman, "I've never met a perfect person before." Judging from the attitude of the people at the party, not many seemed to agree with her attained perfection.

They all had been involved in a long and rather deep discussion on Islam, Buddhism, and Hinduism. As they talked about reaching nirvana, working towards enlightenment, and struggling to attain salvation by one of the four yogas, Shelly, the only Christian, listened attentively. Her mind was reeling. "Can they be serious? Do they really believe this? These are supposedly intelligent people." Then she graciously but boldly entered the conversation. "Have you noticed that all these religions involve humankind reaching or struggling to gain something?"

"Yes, of course," replied one man. "We need to do our part to reach perfection and hope that we have done enough to break the cycle of death and rebirth."

"How do you know when you've done enough?" she asked. The circle of seekers was silent. She continued, "These religions are founded by people who are now dead and never claimed to be God. But they left a number of man-made rules to live by. They say if you follow the 'five pillars' of Islam worship, or the Noble Eightfold Path of Buddhism, or bathe in the Ganges River then maybe, maybe you will reach whatever it is you are supposed to reach. How do you know they work? I find that

Christianity, with Jesus Christ as the founder who claimed to be God, makes a lot more sense. Because of His great love for us, He died for our sins and rose from the dead. He secured eternal salvation for all who believe in what He did on the cross. He claimed to be a personal God very interested and involved in our everyday lives."

Shelly might as well have said that cockroaches were sampling the duck liver pâté. Feet shuffled, eyes rolled, and several people excused themselves from the circle of conversation. Shelly had made a simple comment regarding the person of Jesus Christ. A brave move, no doubt. The remaining people replied, practically in chorus, "Well, we certainly shouldn't be standing around here talking about religion like this!"

"That's strange," Shelly thought. "I could have sworn we already were."

It was perfectly all right to discuss Buddha or Mohammed, but don't try to mention Jesus. There's something about that name. There's power in the name of Jesus. People react, are convicted, and become uncomfortable. They don't want to be reminded that there is a God to whom they will be accountable. It's so much easier to be their own God, follow a set of man-made rules, and hope for the best. Anyway death is surely a long way off.

Shelly made a courageous move that many of us might never consider. She seized the moment. The gospel was shared. Her strong stand drew the attention of one in that circle. Karen thought Christianity made a lot more sense to her as well. She had questions. Shelly could provide some answers. They talked, they exchanged phone numbers, and a significant spiritual transaction with God began that night.

Social gatherings provide excellent opportunities for "name dropping" the person of Jesus Christ at just the right moment. Next time you're at a party drop the "Name above all names" and watch what happens. But be prepared because although some will refuse to hear any more, others may want to know more.

Moody Bible Institute provides good resource material on world religions. Pamphlets called *The Spirit of Truth* and *The Spirit of Error 1* and *2* are concise, good for quick reference, and available in most Christian bookstores. We need to know how to confront the deception that some are believing. The best knowledge, however, is a firm understanding of the Scriptures. When you know the truth, error leaps out in front of you like a truck out of control.

## *Baby Shower Party*

Our words must be matched by our actions. I want to give you one final example of how rubbing shoulders with nonbelievers can leave them with the "aroma of Christ."

Trisha was unmarried and in a crisis pregnancy. We didn't condone what Trisha had done, but we loved her dearly and knew she needed support more than ever. So we decided to have a baby shower for Trisha because we wanted her and all who attended to know that we supported her decision to have the baby. We had a reason to have a party. We were celebrating life!

The real talent and world-class party planner behind it was my friend Carol Cook. From the very beginning the printers must have wondered about the unusual party invitations that read "Life, what a beautiful choice!" The theme was bunnies. I've never seen so many rabbits, bunnies, and furry creatures in all my life. Carrots in little clay pots served as centerpieces. Carol had a field day with her God-given gift of hospitality. Over fifty women attended, including many nonbelievers.

Before Trisha opened the gifts, I prepared a blessing for Andrew, Trisha's son-to-be. I wanted to paint a verbal picture of a special future for them and confirm a blessing on Andrew by an active commitment. I stood, placed my hand on Trisha's tummy, and gave "The Blessing for Drew:"

> Andrew James, surely you will be a blessing to this
>     world that you are soon to enter.
> May you grow tall and strong like an oak tree.
> My you learn to bend and be flexible as a willow.
> May you honor your mother with an obedient heart.
> May you honor God with an obedient spirit.
> May you reach out with your best to the needy.
> May you reach for the highest and best that God has for
>     you.
> May your friends be true and enemies be few.
> May you add joy, peace, beauty, and order to this world.
> May you pursue that which is good in the eyes of the
>     Lord.
> May you find love and acceptance wherever life's path
>     takes you.
> May your sufferings be few and your laughter abundant.
> May you grow to be a man of truth, dignity, and honor.

May you grow to be a man after God's own heart.

May you never forget your mother's love.

Those of us present here today will remember this day
    and this time before your birth. Some of us will walk
    closely by your side in the days, weeks, and years to
    come.

We expectantly await your arrival.

We commit to love, encourage, and pray for you.

May God lavish His blessings upon you.

Andrew James, we all welcome you to the world.

I then closed in prayer. Not too many dry eyes after that.
What do you imagine the nonbelievers thought of this celebra-
tion? They were flabbergasted! Some said, "I can't believe that
Christian women would do this. Aren't they supposed to con-
demn women who have babies out of wedlock?" "How they love
and support her!" "Look how tenderly Judy, her mother, loves
her. My mother would kill me." "I didn't know Christian women
had this much fun." "Could you believe that blessing for the
baby?" "These women really care."

Though the gospel was never presented, all saw it in action.
Christ's love was being manifested through believers who love
one another. That message was silently shouted that sunny afternoon by the hugs, kisses, prayers, and laughter. God is love, and
all who were there witnessed that truth. This party was indeed
showing the way to the Father.

Do you need to give a party to celebrate life, to lift someone's
burden, to stand as a living witness to the nonbelievers? Celebrate your aunt's ninetieth birthday, or the completion of a

friend's chemotherapy, or the birth of a precious baby. Celebrate Jesus' love and give a party for one who needs encouragement. Invite those nonbelievers. Let them witness how we love. You'll arouse their interest.

## The Heavenly Party

There is going to be a party to end all parties at the wedding feast of the Lamb. The Bible says, "Blessed are those who are invited to the wedding supper of the Lamb!" (Revelation 19:9). We don't know what it's going to be like. But this I know for sure: Jesus puts on the best parties! "No eye has seen, nor ear has heard, no mind has conceived what God has prepared for those who love him" (1 Corinthians 2:9). Jesus will have invited the untouchables, the ignored, the lost who were found, Gentiles and Jews, tax collectors, and taxpayers. He will have invited those who have acknowledged their need of Him and those who have placed their faith in Him. The guest list is sure to be nothing short of amazing!

I intend to do my part to add to the guest list. How about you? Share the good news of the Good Shepherd. So many are lost. Tell them of the One who will lead them home to the Father. Gather in the lost, the lonely, the coarse, the unlikely, the irreligious, and the New Ager who stand at the great wooden gates of our household of faith. They are dying for lack of the Bread of Life and the Fountain of Living Water. Then celebrate with Jesus as the true life of the party.

## HOOKS TO HANG YOUR HAT ON

- Isn't it time you invited a nonbeliever to your church, your Bible study, or your Christian party?

- Decide to start thinking about people as Jesus does. No one is "untouchable." Begin by praying for salvation for an "untouchable" that has crossed your path.

- Examine your life. Are you living in a "holy huddle"?

- Throw an evangelistic dinner party. Invite the tax collectors.

- Plan some ice breakers or questions to ask that would prompt deeper discussion than work, children, or the weather.

- Ask, "Lord, if you were me, what would You do in my little corner of the world?"

- Ask a nonbeliever about his or her life philosophy. Ask what is the authority for the beliefs.

- Pray for a boldness to share your belief in Christ.

- Be a "name dropper" of Jesus Christ.

- Be prepared to answer a New Ager with the truth of Scripture. Read *Out on a Broken Limb* by F. LaGard Smith to understand better how to reply to that belief system.

## ALL THINGS CONSIDERED

1. In what ways does the church isolate itself from nonbelievers?

2. What steps can we take to change that perception?

3. How have you personally isolated yourself from nonbelievers? What are you going to do about it? How are you reaching out to your party of three?

4. What makes a believer unapproachable in the eyes of a non-Christian?

5. What steps can you personally take to make yourself more approachable, especially to your party of three, without compromising your walk with Christ?

6. "A man with leprosy came to him and begged him on his knees, 'If you are willing, you can make me clean.' Filled with compassion, Jesus reached out his hand and touched the man. 'I am willing,' he said. 'Be clean!' Immediately the leprosy left him and he was cured" (Mark 1:40–42). What amazing thing did Jesus do before healing the leper? What does this tell us about Jesus? In what sense are we all lepers? How has Jesus touched you?

7. "After this, Jesus went out and saw a tax collector by the name of Levi sitting at his tax booth. 'Follow me,' Jesus said to him, and Levi got up, left everything and followed him" (Luke 5:27–28). What qualified Matthew (Levi) as a disciple? Are you a disciple of Jesus Christ? What is God asking you to set aside in order to follow Him? What will it cost you? Will others notice, as with Matthew?

8. "Then Levi held a great banquet for Jesus at his house, and a large crowd of tax collectors and others were eating with them. But the Pharisees and the teachers of the law who belonged to their sect complained to his disciples, 'Why do you eat and drink with tax collectors and "sinners"?'" (Luke 5:29–30). How do you think the other disciples felt about Jesus choosing Matthew, a hated tax collector, as a disciple? How do you think they felt about the religious leaders' complaint?

9. What would be your attitude if a former prostitute, adulteress, or tax collector-type person joined your Bible study or Sunday school class? What practical things could be done to welcome him or her? How would Jesus welcome that person?

10. We are called to live in the world but not be of the world, to be with sinners but not become complicated with their sins. How can we do this? What do we do to protect ourselves from the sin, yet love the sinner?

# CHAPTER SIX

# WITNESSING IN THE CRISES OF LIFE

*God, it has been said, does not comfort us to make us comfortable, but to make us comforters.*

W. T. PURKISER

Bishop Fulton J. Sheen was visiting a leper hospital in India. As he walked among the patients, he took a moment with each to pray. He was especially moved by one desperately sick man with oozing wounds and a putrid stench. Bishop Sheen stopped, looked upon him with pity in his heart, and walked to his bedside. While leaning over to pray for this leprous man, Bishop Sheen's neck chain broke, and his gold cross dropped from the chain and fell into a particularly hideous open sore in the middle of the man's chest.

Bishop Sheen looked in horror at the situation and paused to decide how to handle it. He admitted later that his first thought was "Well...I'll leave it there and give it to him." But then came that unmistakable still, small voice: "Are you willing to enter into the wounds of others and pick up your cross for My sake?" That profound message took his breath away as he made a life-changing decision. Bishop Sheen said, "When I reached into the weeping wound to take up the cross, my life took on a whole new depth of meaning."[1]

Our paths take us often into the wounds of the world. They may not assail our nostrils with their stench nor repulse us with their appearance; nonetheless the hidden diseases of the heart are ever present. If we could but see the invisible, we would witness the sores, the lesions, the abscesses that are eating away at people's lives. It's called sin.

May our prayer be, "Oh Father, give me Your eyes that I might see them as You do." If we truly could see with our Father's eyes, within even the least of these we would find the image of God. Would we act any differently if we could see Jesus reflected back to us in the faces of the sick and dying?

People in pain are often the most open to the gospel. Their reserves are gone; their human strength has dissipated; their future is uncertain and frightening. Now they must admit they no longer have control over their lives. It is then many nonbelievers realize they have come to the end of themselves. Hopefully we are there to tell them about the only One who will give them a life that is eternal, a peace the world cannot give, and an unconditional love in their darkest, loneliest moments. This requires risk, courage, and a willingness to move out of our comfort zone for the name of Christ.

### Be a Woman of Courage in the Face of Crisis

During the reign of Ahasuerus (Xerxes), King of Persia (486–465 B.C.), there lived a courageous Jewish woman named Esther.

King Ahasuerus had become smitten by her beauty, and Esther was crowned his queen. Not long afterward an evil man named Haman, who was in a powerful position of leadership, issued a decree to slaughter all the Jews in Ahasuerus's kingdom. Mordecai, Esther's cousin, convinced her to be bold spirited and approach the king, pleading on behalf of the Jews. Mordecai told her, "And who knows but that you have come to royal position for such a time as this?" (Esther 4:14).

However, this was dangerous business indeed because royal law prohibited anyone from appearing before the king without prior invitation. The penalty was death unless the king extended the golden scepter. When Esther came before the king, he received her with favor. Through a series of events she revealed the plot to the king, Haman was hanged, and the annihilation of Jews was averted. The exciting, gripping account is found in the book of Esther in the Old Testament.

Surely God had planned for Esther to rise to her royal position to save the Jews from death. She was given a high position for a high calling. God has great plans for us too. We have royal blood into which we were born spiritually. We are sons and daughters of the King of kings, princes and princesses, created for a great purpose—the high calling to speak boldly of the One who saves from eternal death.

Ministering to nonbelievers in their illness requires a special measure of courage. We're often afraid of offending or causing further distress. After all, like Esther, we're discussing life and death, and many don't want to face the obvious. But it's only a matter of time before the opportunity will present itself. We will either be the caregiver, a spectator of a caregiving situation, or the recipient of a caregiver—we will either be beside the bed, at the foot of the bed, or in the bed. Did you ever consider these circumstances as prime opportunities for sharing the good news and the love of Jesus Christ? They are among the best, but it will require courage to face sickness, pain, and death.

Some believers have God-given spiritual gifts of ministering to the sick, injured, depressed, dying, or elderly. In their nurturing and compassion they exemplify Christlike character. While it's the most natural thing in the world for those so gifted, for many of us these opportunities can be awkward and distressing. Yet we bring encouragement with our visits. We bring comfort with our pot of chicken soup and delight with a phone call. We bring love in the name of Christ with a soft pillow to cradle their heads. In the process many opportunities present themselves to share the hope that is within us. May we who are of royal blood be so privileged. Let us face these spiritual and physical life-and-death situations with the courage of Esther.

## Give Intensive Care

We know that the unbeliever's greatest need is to be reconciled to God through faith in Jesus Christ. But we need somehow to enter their physical pain and emotional hurt as best we can to understand and meet them where they are. It's like watching a marathon race and having your legs ache for the runners at the five-mile mark. How can we empathize and identify with needy people to reach them for Christ?

I was watching the news one evening when I heard a wonderful example of meeting people where they are. In Oceanside, California, a fifth-grade class at Lake Elementary School identified with a friend. Ian O'Gorman's buddies didn't want him to have to endure the embarrassment of his chemotherapy alone. They didn't want him to feel as though he didn't fit in. So with their parents' approval all thirteen of his friends went down to the barbershop together and had their heads shaved. When they were all bald, people didn't know who had the cancer. The boys' teacher was so moved he even shaved his head!

I'm not proposing we do the same for our friends who are going through chemotherapy, but I am suggesting we be as willing to step into another's shoes. If these boys were to share Jesus Christ with Ian, I have an inkling he would give his full attention. What do you think? How far beyond our comfort zones will we go to reach out to hurting people and show them Christ's love?

"People don't really care how much you know until they know how much you care. There is a direct correlation between the assurance of love and the acceptance of truth."[2] One of the key issues in witnessing is entering into a meaningful relationship with our nonbelieving friends. There is no one set of rules or drumbeat to march to. But there is one common denominator. Love them. Seek to discover how you can communicate that love to them. Before they ever listen to you as you share the gospel, take time to listen to them, meet them where they are, and love them in the process. This "intensive care" may give them a listening, receptive ear to the gospel of Jesus Christ. And you may have the privilege to tell it.

### Don't Overlook the Power of a Touch

What power there is in the human touch—an embrace of comfort, a shoulder to cry on, the dressing of a wound, or holding the hand of one in need. Jesus physically touched lepers, the blind, the lame, the terminally ill. He did so to heal them, but our hands can minister healing and comfort as well.

Stuart's son, Jason, was mentally disabled. Though he had the body of a seventeen-year-old, he had the mind of a five-year-old. He was so open, so transparent, so free with his affections. He was loved deeply, and he loved unabashedly in return.

Stuart took Jason everywhere with him. When Stuart's teenage daughter broke her arm, Jason accompanied them to the emergency room. While Stuart was in with his daughter, Jason stayed in the waiting room. The room was empty except for one elderly man, who appeared to be a street person. He was smelly and ragged from his cap to his coat to his cuffs.

Upon returning to the waiting room, Stuart found Jason with his arm around the old man, who was now weeping uncontrollably. "I'm very sorry," said Stuart. "Has my son offended you in some way?"

Through his tears the man replied, "Oh no, it's just that I haven't been hugged like this since my mother held me as a baby in her arms." Jason understood in his simple way what a privilege it was to hold the head of one created in the image of God.

Have you cradled your mother's head on her death bed? Have you held a suffering child? Have you wrapped your love around your spouse as he or she was slipping off into eternity? Have you wiped the brow of your terminally ill best friend? Then indeed you have touched an image-bearer of God. What if we were given one of the greatest privileges, like that of holding the head of Jesus as Mary did? We have been given that privilege with everyone we comfort. As we reach out to touch and to comfort perhaps walls of resistance will break down and a path will open for us to share the gospel.

## Provide Practical Support

How can we, under these special circumstances, express Christ's love to the nonbeliever? Think of a time when you were ill, depressed, or stressed out. What would have communicated love to you? What did you wish others would do? What practical things could they have done on your behalf? Did you need a short but comforting visit? Perhaps it was an errand to be done, laundry to be washed, phone calls to be made, or children to be cared for. Maybe you would have loved a book to help pass the time, or someone to drive you to the doctor.

I came across a book by Erica Levy Klein entitled *201 Things to Do While You're Getting Better.* I can't endorse everything in the book, but she does come up with some great ideas. How about spending time with sick friends playing Scrabble or chess? Or give them a Zolo II, an incredible, put-it-together-yourself, adult toy that's never the same twice. Their imagination can go wild with the ninety-five hand-carved wooden pieces that fit together in all kinds of weird ways. Buy them a needlepoint, cross-stitch, or crewel project. Create a tape of encouraging, fun messages from some of their friends, coworkers, or relatives. Suggest they make a list of all the "bests" and "worsts" in their lives—the best movies, the worst vacation, the best Christmas, the worst meal, the best book, the worst camping trip, the best birthday, the worst date. Share common experiences from your past—first date, blind dates, graduations, weddings, births, or learning how to drive, roller-skate, or ski.

When we've helped them pass the time by just being there, we might also have the privilege of reading a passage from an inspirational book. Who knows, they may even agree to a verse or two from the Bible. These are golden opportunities to demonstrate the love of Christ by being available, and they may open doors for the gospel. God will show us what we can uniquely do to communicate love to them. He's got lots of terrific ideas. Just ask Him.

## *Pray for Opportunities*

Several years ago the church we attended in Palo Alto, California, had an informal service called Body Life, which met on Sunday nights. One evening during prayer requests a young woman stood up and asked for prayers for her close friend, a paraplegic, who was in intensive care at Stanford Hospital. Ron Ritchie, one of the pastors, led the congregation in prayer for this woman, who was a nonbeliever. He prayed for someone to witness to her as she lay in her hospital bed, perhaps a nurse or another patient in the same room.

Early Monday morning Anne Marie, Ron's wife, went to Stanford Hospital for some tests because of kidney problems. But before they could do the procedure, they checked her tolerance for iodine by giving her a few drops. Anne Marie said, "I began to sneeze uncontrollably, then I became very cold, my speech became slurred, and I couldn't feel or move my body. I didn't just pass out; I lost all of my vital signs. The medical team called out, 'She's gone!' Later I concluded God wasn't ready for me yet because I was revived not once but twice that morning." Billy Crystal said in the movie *The Princess Bride* that there are two kinds of dead: "mostly dead" and "all dead." Anne Marie would tell you she was "all dead," twice!

"Guess where they put me?" she said. "Right next to the young woman my husband had prayed for. We were in intensive care together for two life-transforming days. Of course I shared Jesus with her. And on that bed, with her heart wonderfully warmed by the truth, the young woman trusted her life to Jesus Christ. This baby Christian ended up going to Bible college, meeting a wonderful paraplegic man, and marrying him. All because of a few drops of iodine and the power of prayer."

God doesn't waste anything in His economy, does He? You may be a bedridden believer, but your life is not over. Others may be watching, waiting, and wondering if Jesus is a living reality in your life. "And who knows but that you have come to royal position for such a time as this?"

## Hospice—Final Exit Care

Cathy Brown is a Christian and an RN Case Manager for Hospice of the Valley here in Phoenix. Her total focus is on the terminally ill. She goes into patients' homes to provide symptom management for pain, nausea, vomiting, or whatever their problem may be in order to make them as comfortable and as autonomous as possible in their last days. Cathy has been given permission in her work to share Christ if the opportunity presents itself. One might think this is morbid work, but Cathy is fun loving and absolutely delighted with her calling. And indeed it is a calling.

"I don't feel comfortable witnessing," Cathy says, "unless I know the people will not reject me and are totally safe to approach." (Can you relate?) "Also, I like to have things organized and controlled. What an enormous lesson I had to learn in this work. I learned to approach even the 'unsafe.' I came to understand that if they rebelled against the gospel message they were rejecting Christ, not me. And I quickly discovered I could not be in control. It is not my agenda but God's."

Cathy says, "I've always felt comfortable around and interested in people who were dying and facing the last great challenge of their lives. We put so much energy and preparation into people who are planning a birth, graduation, or a wedding. I believe we need to put quality time and energy into people who are dying as well. It gives us an understanding of the value, fragility, and mortality of our own lives. Every family member, friend, and caregiver needs to serve that person and honor him or her."

Cathy told me of one of her patients who was in her seventies and claimed to be a Christian. "She read the Bible, prayed daily, and attended church regularly. One day as I sat with her, I said, 'Things are getting real close now, and you'll be going to heaven soon. How does that make you feel?' She replied, 'Well I don't know if I'm going to heaven. I *hope* I've been good enough.'

"I thought, 'Hope you've been good enough? We need to do some work here.' When I want to better understand where people are in their spiritual journey, I gently question them about their beliefs. I will often ask permission before I delve into deeper things. I might say, 'Help me understand what you believe. May I ask you some questions about your spiritual life? Who is God to you? What do you believe about Him? Does He impact your life in some way?' These are fairly nonthreatening questions. I also ask them specifically if they believe in Jesus Christ rather than if they are Christians. Some people think they're Christians if they live in America and don't sacrifice animals!

"I shared with my dear patient that the Bible says it isn't how good we've been that earns us heaven. It's placing our belief and trust in Jesus Christ for our eternal destiny. Eternal life is a gift; we don't earn it.

"I asked her, 'May I pray for you?' and then went through the four spiritual laws in my prayer. I prayed that she would know God loved her and wanted her to know Him personally through Jesus Christ. I said we all have sinned, are separated from God, and need to ask forgiveness. And finally I prayed she would receive Jesus as Savior and Lord and know for certain where she would spend eternity.

"I told her, 'I'm going to be praying for you today that before nightfall you will *know* where you're going to spend eternity. When I come tomorrow, you're going to say, 'Praise the Lord, I'm going to heaven!' Till then I want you to pray for me so that I will know better how to pray for you.'

"The next day as I walked in, she pointed to the sky. 'What does that mean?' I asked. 'I'm going to heaven!' she replied. 'I didn't sleep much last night. I kept thinking about all you said and what we prayed about. And now I know for certain I'm going to heaven!'

"I asked if she felt comfortable enough to talk to her sons about her prayer and decision. Figuring we were on a roll, I wanted to take advantage of every opportunity. A short time later before she went into a coma, her sons arrived. I asked them, 'Did you have a chance to talk to your mother before she went into the coma?' 'Yes,' the younger one replied. 'Mom was...well, I don't quite know how to express it. I guess I'd say "free." I've never seen her happy like that before.' 'Did she tell you why?' I asked. They said, 'She told us you prayed with her.'

"I then went on to tell them what we prayed about. I went through the plan of salvation. (I was getting good at this.) After all, they wanted to know some of their mother's last words. And when I told them she knew she was going to heaven, it seemed to comfort them. I'd like to tell you they repented on the spot and gave their lives to Jesus. It didn't happen, at least not then. But they did listen, and perhaps one day they will remember some of the last words of their mother and trust Christ with their own lives."

It's never too late in others' lives to reach out to them. Here was a woman in her seventies who never had anyone share what a relationship with Jesus Christ meant. Her greatest need at the time was to know it meant eternal security. She died a few days later secure in that knowledge.

Is there someone in our lives that desperately needs to hear this good news? What are we waiting for? The perfect moment? It's too late if we wait for the memorial service. But remember to ask permission and answer their questions gently. Then perhaps they're ready for the good news of Jesus Christ. "And who knows but that you have come to royal position for such a time as this?"

## Spiritual Assessment

Cathy put together a list of spiritual assessment questions she asks her patients in order to determine their spiritual temperature. Even though Cathy witnesses mainly to patients who are near death, we can take note. The tools she uses can be applied with the seriously ill or the healthy.

1. Is there anything that brings you peace and comfort spiritually?
2. Do you have spiritual support?
3. Who is your spiritual support? A friend, pastor, relative?
4. What is the source of your strength right now?
5. Has your illness raised any questions about life?
6. What part does God play in your life?
7. Do you think that knowing God in a personal way would help you?
8. Has your illness changed your view of God?
9. How would you describe God?
10. In what way is your faith important to you right now?
11. Is prayer important to you? In what way?
12. Is the Bible or any other book helpful to you? How?
13. What helps you most when you feel afraid or alone?
14. What do you do in a crisis?
15. Would you like me to pray with you or read the Bible to you?

Cathy gives her patients homework assignments with these questions. When she returns for a visit, they discuss one or two of them. Many of these questions are nonthreatening and provide wonderful openers for people in stressful situations.

## Not All Endings Are Happy Endings

Cathy had another patient in her late seventies—a wealthy and once-beautiful woman who didn't have long to live. The woman's son told Cathy, "She has never believed in God. I doubt she ever will. I wouldn't discuss it with her at all." Cathy questioned further, "What if she brings up spiritual matters? Would it be all right then to talk to her about God?" And he consented.

As Cathy and the woman were sitting together in her garden one day, Cathy asked her, "What do you think about when you sit out here?" She said, "Today I was thinking about creation." Cathy thought, "Terrific. What better place to start than Genesis." Her patient continued, "I believe God created all of this, and I believe He created man and woman as well." Cathy couldn't help but think, "And her son said she didn't believe in God!"

Cathy decided to ask her some of the spiritual assessment questions she had compiled, so she said, "Who is God?" The lady thought for a moment then said, "Well, He's a creator." "Does He have any meaning for you?" Cathy asked. "No, I don't really think so" came her reply. "Then let me ask you this," said Cathy. "What do you think is the purpose of man and woman on earth? Why do you think He created us?"

The next few moments of conversation were so unbelievable they will be imprinted on Cathy's mind for a long time. The woman began, "Oh that's easy. God created us so we could find our own purpose. The purpose is different for everyone. My purpose in life has been twofold: fast cars and high fashion. I have always driven fast sports cars, and I have always loved and worn high fashion."

The woman had lost over a hundred pounds. Now fifty pounds, her skin stretched over a bony frame. Weakness had overtaken her so she could no longer put her foot to the pedal and peel away in her sports cars. No more dress-up. No more hot cars. No more purpose to life.

Cathy asked, "Do you want to talk about it?" "What is there to talk about?" she replied. "My life is over. It was over the day I was diagnosed with this illness. What else is there in life? My two purposes have been taken from me, and I have nothing left."

Cathy tried to refocus her. "We just talked about God, creation, and purpose in life. Did you ever consider that perhaps fast cars and high fashion were not why you were created? That maybe that was not God's intended purpose for your life?" The woman questioned, "Why else would I be here on earth?" Cathy asked her, "Do you believe in heaven?" Her quick retort was biting. "Absolutely not! This is all there is."

Cathy said, "Oh my goodness. I would be so depressed if I believed that. May I tell you about my God who comforts in times such as this, who gives us a higher purpose in life, who desires that we spend all of eternity with Him in heaven, who envelopes us in His love and protection? May I?" With an icy chill in her voice, the patient simply said, "No, I don't want to hear about Him. I'm not really interested."

The next day in her anger, bitterness, and loneliness the woman died. Cathy felt burdened with a sense of failure. Then she remembered she wasn't responsible for her patient's salvation. That was between the woman and a sovereign God. The Holy Spirit was in charge, not Cathy. She had to let it go. The living still needed to be witnessed to; the woman's son, daughter-in-law, and grandchildren all believed as she did. Cathy's work was not over. "And who knows but that you have come to royal position for such a time as this?"

Why do we include a story like this in a book on witnessing? Because not every encounter is a success story. Not every nonbeliever will be open to hear the gospel. Not everyone will die with the anticipation of a heavenly reward with Jesus. Doors will be shut in our faces. People will tell us to get out of their lives. Hearts will seal tight at the mention of Jesus. We seek to comfort the ill, the dying, the depressed, and the disabled, but some will refuse to be comforted. People will be rebellious and defiant in the face of God's Word. The message is not always welcomed nor, I might add, is the messenger.

We must be responsible for the truth of the gospel that has been given to us, but we are not responsible for what nonbelievers do with it. When they don't want to pursue spiritual things, we must respect their stand. Perhaps God will draw them and one day they will come to us and open up the conversation. We must allow God to do His perfect work, always remembering He gave people the gift of free will.

Our fast-cars-and-high-fashion nonbeliever exercised her free will. She chose to reject Him. For those who don't want God and certainly don't want to spend eternity with Him, God created a place called hell where they never have to see Him. Men and women choose hell; God doesn't choose it for them. "He [God] is patient with you, not wanting anyone to perish, but everyone to come to repentance" (2 Peter 3:9).

## Faith in the Midst of Our Troubles

"This journal," Heidi wrote, "is a collection of dates, events, thoughts, and reactions to the discovery of a brainstem tumor in our precious boy, James. May these pages be a testimony to God's faithfulness and grace during this devastating trial." She then recorded Isaiah 55:8–9: "'For my thoughts are not your thoughts, neither are your ways my ways,' declares the Lord. 'As the heavens are higher than the earth, so are my ways higher than your ways and my thoughts than your thoughts.'"

"James was seven years old when his brainstem tumor was diagnosed. I used to think a brain tumor was one of the worst things that could happen. Then Michael and I had to face it with our own son.

"We believe God gave us His perspective on this. We didn't shake our fists at Him and scream 'Why us?' as if we have a right to have perfectly healthy children who live to a ripe old age. Every day we live is a gift. You hear a lot of people say, 'You've just got to get through it. Grit your teeth and face it.' We want to say to them, 'No, that's not it! It's God's faithfulness and grace. It's the truth of Scripture.' We knew we could never get through it on our own strength. Our prayer was that God would use us to show others where we received our strength.

"God used James's brain tumor and our lives as a testimony to His faithfulness. We discovered we had a platform. We had suffered, we had wept, and people would listen. People did listen. The verse that was foremost in our minds and hearts during this trial was 1 Peter 3:15: 'Always be prepared to give an answer to everyone who asks you to give the reason for the hope that you have. But do this with gentleness and respect.'

"God brought the Body of Christ together in our local church as a result of our trial. For example, the day of the surgery our church kept a constant prayer vigil. Every fifteen minutes a number of people would either come to the church or pray where they were. Christians saw this as an opportunity to get their own children involved in prayer. What a profound witness to these young children to see their parents on their knees praying for another child.

"About twenty-five people came to the hospital to pray and support us. They literally filled the waiting room. People took off from work and stayed the entire eight hours of surgery. The nurses who came out every forty-five minutes to let us know how things were going couldn't help but notice this incredibly caring group of people. As the family of God operates with the love of Christ, especially in a highly visible trial like this one, the world notices. What a testimony.

"My husband's secretary bought a book for James called *My Hospital Book* by William Coleman. The nurses wrote notes in it to James and signed it. And lots of our Christian friends signed it with verses, notes of spiritual encouragement, and reminders of God's faithfulness. So when nonbelievers saw it, and many did, they had the opportunity to read the scriptures and see how the Bible is so relevant. It opened great opportunities for spiritual discussion.

"We discovered that people will often talk about God and prayer in times such as this, but we felt a real burden to clarify just what God we were talking about. This of course led us to speak about Scripture. Many nonbelievers just make up their own God as they go along in life. They have no source of truth, no standard to look to. We saw that prayer was certainly not an exclusive indicator of knowing the Lord. Lots of nonbelievers said they were praying.

"A woman whose son was losing the battle with cancer happened to be on James' floor. She was very angry at God. Her mental picture of the Lord was a mean, uncaring, ill-humored, and wrathful God. 'Why did He do this to my son? When I get to heaven, He'll have to give an account of why He did this!' she demanded. I let her 'unpack' all her complaints and hurts. But she wasn't open to see God's love, care, or compassion. In her eyes He wasn't demonstrating unconditional love at all. Perhaps when her son is gone, I'll have an opportunity to share Christ, so I'm maintaining contact with her.

"Then there was the woman in my brain tumor support group who lost her four-year-old son to cancer. I witnessed to her after the funeral and told her about God's true character as revealed in the Bible. I told her that He never suspends one attribute to exercise another, that He is at the same time the lover of our souls and righteous Judge, the Life-Giver and the One who removes our last breath of life. I explained that His perfect character never changes, His unconditional love is ever constant, and He is the only source of peace and comfort in our suffering. I know the Holy Spirit was working mightily because she agreed to meet with me on a regular basis for a Bible study. I had earned the right to be heard because she saw my faith lived out through our sea of troubles.

"The night after surgery we received the news that the tumor was benign. We would have our son back! The Lord answered all of our requests. James would not be physically deficient. That night as I went to my knees in prayer, I wrote in my journal, 'Let me never forget the grace, Lord, that You lavished on us this day.'

"James's surgery was in January, and on March 1 we brought him to church. When our pastor announced, 'James Jacoby is with us today,' the entire church stood and clapped for our little son but most of all for God's faithfulness."

Heidi and Michael Jacoby's lives were a striking testimony to all who witnessed their trial. Family, physicians, nurses, teachers, James's classmates—everyone saw the gospel lived out. We know God does not always choose to heal physically. Yet in His sovereignty He chose to heal James. Though his prognosis is uncertain, Heidi and Michael take one day at a time and continue to speak about Jesus to anyone who asks about the hope they have.

Maybe this day finds us bedridden, perhaps even facing death. What purpose can we find for our illness? Is it needless suffering? Or, is it possible that God wants to use us even now in our weakness to show His strength? Can we not tell our wayward children, relatives, friends, "There is purpose in every breath I take. The Lord has lengthened my days for just such a moment as this. May I tell you about my God who will soon greet me as I move from this life into the next? He is loving, forgiving, tender, and full of grace. He delivers the captives from sin. He sympathizes and saves, strengthens and sustains. He guards and guides. And one day he will ultimately heal me when I see Him face to face. Do you know Him? May I tell you about Him?"

"And who knows but that you have come to royal position for such a time as this?"

## HOOKS TO HANG YOUR HAT ON

- We must minister to nonbelievers' immediate physical needs before we can address their spiritual ones.

- Remember your royal position and your high calling for such a time as you may be facing.

- People don't really care how much we know until they know how much we care.

- Seek to discover how you are able to communicate love to them.

- Visit the sick, run an errand, wash their clothes, take their children on an outing. Play Scrabble, chess, or some other game they might enjoy. Read a well-chosen book to them. Ask yourself, "What would I like done if I were ill?"

- Pick up a copy of the Four Spiritual Laws at your Christian bookstore.

- Ask permission before you delve deeply into others' spiritual lives.

- *Gently* question them about their beliefs.

- Select a few of the spiritual assessment questions
  you think would be good for your situation.
  Memorize them, then use them.

- If you're feeling inadequate, write down everything
  you want to say.
  Then practice until it becomes heart knowledge.

- Memorize Esther 4:14 for your own encouragement.

## ALL THINGS CONSIDERED

1. Are you uncomfortable around the sick and dying? Why or why not? Do you avoid personal contact with them? What would Jesus have you do?

2. Have you ever been in great physical pain? What brought you comfort? What helped you pass the time? What did you think about?

3. Did your illness change your view of God? Do you look at life differently as a result? How?

4. Have you ever had the privilege of sharing Jesus with a sick or dying person? What did you say? How did you open the conversation? What was the result?

5. Write out the steps of the Four Spiritual Laws. Underline the action verbs. Now repeat the steps to yourself using the verbs as an aid.

6. What is your purpose in life in the light of Scripture? How are you practically fulfilling it?

7. Gleaning from the following verses, what would you say to someone who hoped they might be good enough to enter heaven?

"If you confess with your mouth, 'Jesus is Lord,' and believe in your heart that God raised him from the dead, you will be saved. For it is with your heart that you believe and are justified, and it is with your mouth that you confess and are saved." (Romans 10:9–10)

"And this is the testimony: God has given us eternal life, and this life is in his Son. He who has the Son has life; he who does not have the Son of God does not have life." (1 John 5:11–12)

"For it is by grace you have been saved, through faith— and this not from yourselves, it is the gift of God—not by works, so that no one can boast." (Ephesians 2:8–9)

8. "And who knows but that you have come to royal position for such a time as this?" (Esther 4:14). Share a time when you were well aware that God had uniquely brought you to a particular situation and place for His purposes. Does knowing that you are of royal position (a child of the King of kings) give you confidence to speak for His name's sake? Why?

9. If you were on your death bed and had just enough breath to share Jesus with one person, who would it be? What would you tell him or her?

10. How were you personally challenged by this chapter? What are you going to do about it?

# CHAPTER SEVEN

# SOLDIERS ON A MISSION FROM GOD

*"Therefore go and make disciples of all nations, baptizing them in the name of the Father and of the Son and of the Holy Spirit, and teaching them to obey everything I have commanded you."*

MATTHEW 28:19–20

T his is not the army I signed up for!"

A smooth-talking army recruiter had painted a rosy picture of luxury condos and yacht-filled harbors to a spoiled and pampered young lady. He convinced her the army was just what she needed for security, a new life, a good dose of self-confidence, and a three-year, all-expenses-paid tour. When the recruiter said, "We'll get you in the best physical shape you've ever been in," she figured it would be like three years at La Costa Resort and Spa!

The first day of basic training quickly dispelled the illusion.

We can laugh at this fictional dilemma of Goldie Hawn in *Private Benjamin,* but as a soldier of Christ have you ever felt the same way? Have there been days when you thought, "Lord, this is not the tour of duty I signed up for." We didn't know that becoming spiritually mature would require so much courage, endurance, perseverance, and commitment. Why, we're even issued armor for battle! Why are we so surprised? We shouldn't be; after all we're on a mission from God.

Let's take a moment and consider this mission. We're fighting an enemy greater than ourselves, serving a commander in chief we cannot see, for a cause we cannot measure, and a reward we have to die to get. How does it feel so far? But stick around; the story turns out great. The war has been won!

We represent our commander in chief, Jesus, who is far more powerful than our enemy. He has commanded us to fulfill a special mission, the Great Commission: "Therefore go and make disciples of all nations, baptizing them in the name of the Father and of the Son and of the Holy Spirit, and teaching them to obey everything I have commanded you" (Matthew 28:19–20). Basically Jesus said, "Look, you're on a mission from God. Do everything I have taught you."

Jesus also said, "You will be my witnesses in Jerusalem, and in all Judea and Samaria, and to the ends of the earth" (Acts 1:8). If I may paraphrase, Jesus is saying, "You will witness about me at home, in your community, in your sphere of influence, in your neighboring countries, and to the uttermost parts of the earth." Going to the ends of the earth is a pretty major goal to fulfill. Jesus is not asking us for any halfhearted or half-baked commitment. It's total involvement.

Jesus didn't say, "Go, and if you feel up to it, perhaps you could make a disciple or two along the way." He also didn't say, "If it's convenient for you, if it doesn't put you out too much, you might consider being My witnesses." He said, "Go; make; baptize; teach; be witnesses to all nations, to the ends of the earth."

We have a wonderful mission to fulfill. But it's so enormous.

And there are so many ways to approach it. How do we personalize it with our unique gifts, talents, abilities, resources, and time? How can the activities of our lives fulfill our mission from God?

## Soldiers with a Mission Statement

Just as God has completely equipped us as Christian soldiers to fulfill the Great Commission, we must believe He will enable us to complete His purpose. We must believe it is doable. We must believe it will have eternal impact. If we don't, we will never give it our full energy and focus. God will provide all we need to fulfill it, but we must understand His unique purpose for us.

I love what exercise does for me, but I don't leap out of bed in the morning, saying, "Wow, three and a half miles on the treadmill. I can hardly wait." Some mornings I wake up footsore and weary eyed, hoping I'll never see another piece of exercise equipment as long as I live. That's when I start thinking, "It's too cold. It's too hot. I'm too pooped. I haven't had my coffee yet. The Stairmaster is too hard, the treadmill too fast, and the weights too heavy." It's at those times—when I'm tired, weary of the routine, and exhausted—that I say to myself, "Tell me again, Roberta. Why are we doing this? What is our purpose for all this hard work? What are our goals?" Then I remember, and I repeat my purpose to myself. This helps tremendously to give me strength and determination.

When we wake up in the morning, do we ask ourselves, "What is my purpose today? Lord, how should I order my day? What should I do? What should I stop doing? Should I commit myself to this project or that cause? How can I best use my time, abilities, resources, spiritual gifts, and personality traits to be a witness for Jesus Christ? Tell me again, Lord, why am I doing this?" Our actions will spring from our purpose, so we need to ask ourselves, "What is the big purpose of my life?"

Companies devise strategic goals. Educational institutions have statements of objectives. Football teams have game plans. Military units have missions. If we are soldiers of Christ on a mission from God, then we ought to have a clear idea of our personal mission. Have you ever developed a statement of objectives, a game plan, or a mission statement for your life—a clear and concise statement of your life's purpose and reason for being?

I was first confronted with this idea when someone asked me, "Roberta, don't you have a mission statement for your life outlining how you hope to fulfill the Great Commission? How could a woman with your full and busy life not have a written, well-defined, well-thought-out purpose to her life?" Good question. I simply thought everything I did had a purpose. I prayed about my decisions. I sought God. I searched His Word. Wasn't that enough?

Jesus' life was disciplined by a sense of purpose. He defined His mission when He said, "For the Son of Man came to seek and to save what was lost" (Luke 19:10). Everything Jesus did was in light of fulfilling His mission on Calvary. That was His life's focus. What is ours?

If we do not submit our daily decisions to a mission statement, we will be at the mercy of emergencies, the tyranny of the moment, our weaknesses, and other people's demands. A mission statement is a benchmark against which we measure all of our activities to keep us from being distracted from our life's goals. Because of my mission statement, I am learning to say no to that which is good in order to say yes to that which is excellent, to that which God has called me to do.

As I began drafting my mission statement, I followed Colossians 4:5–6 to help me define my purpose. This was my rather lengthy, original mission statement: "I purpose to prepare myself to be a witness for Christ through my speaking and writing. I purpose that my words may always be seasoned with wisdom and grace, making the most of the opportunity, so that I may know how I should respond to each person with the love of my Lord Jesus Christ and according to His will."

## Preparing a Mission Statement

Before we prepare a mission statement, we need to understand some basics. First it is vital that we understand our identity in Christ, who God says we are. The truest thing about ourselves is what God says. I encourage you to take several names from the list at the end of this chapter and each day during your quiet time look them up in your Bible and read them within the context of the passage. Then meditate on them and think of practical ways to "flesh them out" in your life. We must first know our identity in Christ to be witnesses of His life within us.

If you would like to study this further, I recommend several books. *His Image, My Image* by Josh McDowell deals with a deepening awareness of one's own dignity and purpose as a Christian. He encourages the reader to apply the truth of our identity in Christ. *Victory over Darkness* by Neil T. Anderson studies the power of our identity in Christ and how to stand against the spiritual forces of this world. And of course, I'd recommend *The Me God Sees,* in which I talk of our identity in Christ, how to free ourselves from the burdens of our past, and how to be the people God created us to be in order to be difference makers for Christ.

Second, we must identify our spiritual gifts, as we discussed earlier in the book. Knowing our spiritual gifts helps us to understand our uniqueness and how God wired us to serve Him. This will be the foundation on which we will write our mission statement. Since Jesus' commission to us was to witness, we need to keep that perspective in our mission statement. How have I been equipped to carry out my mission of witnessing? What passion has He given me?

Third, we need to ask someone who knows us well to hold us accountable to our mission statement. At the time I first developed my mission statement, I belonged to an accountability group in which all five of us prepared mission statements. Several times a year we reviewed them and held one another accountable. It helped to keep me focused.

**WHERE TO BEGIN?** So let's begin. Get your pen and paper. We're going to prepare a mission statement together. I know what a difference this has made in my life as a witness for Jesus Christ. I know it can do the same for you if you daily apply it to your life.

Be sure to take a few moments to pray for God's wisdom and direction before you start formulating your statement. You want to know His mind, hear His heartbeat, and listen to His voice.

Be patient. It may take days, weeks, or even months to put it all together, but you are doing something to last a lifetime.

During the entire process search the Scriptures for verses that speak to you of God's purpose for your life. Then allow God to refine your mission statement until you can say, "That's it. I know it to the depth of my being."

As a way to get started, you might want to look at some other people's mission statements:

"That I might show myself faithful to the Lord in all my endeavors."

"That all I do and say be for the glory of God."

"To put into practice whatever I have learned, received, or heard from the Lord."

"To be a godly woman whose life is marked by prayer, obedience, and surrender to Jesus Christ with a gentle and quiet spirit."

"To give God my heart, others my helping hands."

"To honor God daily. To let others see Jesus Christ in me. To keep my priorities in order."

"To spend the rest of my earthly life fulfilling the will of God."

"To choose life." (This woman desires not only to make life-giving choices for herself in her eating, drinking, exercising, fasting, prayer, meditation, and Bible study but to tell others how to choose life in Christ.)

**IT MUST BE REALISTIC.** Consider your time, gifts, talents, abilities, and resources as you begin. My personal desire was to write and speak with the profundity of Max Lucado, the humor of Erma Bombeck, the evangelistic thrust of Billy Graham, the theology of Chuck Swindoll, and the relevancy of Bill Hybels—and for it all to have the touch of Christ's anointed hand. I had to ask myself, "Is that realistic?"

What about you? Where are you going? How do you plan on getting there and witnessing with the time and talents God has given you? Scripture doesn't say not to make plans, but not to arrogantly set goals with no thought of God's will.

**IT MUST BE LONG RANGE.** Our statements need to be big enough to challenge us for a lifetime. Someone once said, "Make no small plans, for they have no capacity to stir men's souls." My desire was to stir souls toward Jesus Christ, and I wanted to do this with wisdom and grace. That was going to take a lifetime.

As you draft your statement, think how you would be challenged for a lifetime. Consider this from Ephesians: "Now to him who is able to do immeasurably more than all we ask or imagine, according to his power that is at work within us" (3:20). As 2 Corinthians 9:8 says: "And God is able to make all grace abound to you, so that in all things at all times, having all that you need, you will abound in every good work." And as Luke says, "From everyone who has been given much, much will be demanded; and from the one who has been entrusted with much, much more will be asked" (12:48).

Make plans as big as the ones God has for you.

**IT MUST BE MEASURABLE DAILY.** Now the glamour of my mission statement took on the nitty-gritty of the daily grind. I would only be deceiving myself if I thought I could fulfill my mission statement and avoid working toward it daily. This is where the rubber of daily decisions meets the road of discipline. Our activities and decisions need to be filtered through the big picture.

If we understand our mission and diligently pursue it, over a period of time there will be fruit—the fruit of the Spirit which is Christlike character. "The fruit of the Spirit is love, joy, peace, patience, kindness, goodness, faithfulness, gentleness and self-control" (Galatians 5:22–23). Then God brings a sense of accomplishment, fulfillment, and delight.

I could measure, in a sense, my fruitfulness as I considered my spiritual growth. Am I more joyful, loving, peaceful, patient than I was last month or last year? Fruitfulness is developing a Christlike character. It is not having "notches" on our Bibles for the people we have led to the Lord. That may be a result, but it's not fruitfulness. "It's not nickels and noses," as my friend Larry Roberts commented. "Nickels and noses?" I questioned. "Yes," he said, "some churches count the nickels and the noses—how many people attended and how much money they collected." That's not the fruitfulness we're talking about.

Include in your draft some measurable, daily actions.

**IT MUST BE SPECIFIC.** One of my desires was to reach the lost for Jesus Christ through my writing and speaking, responding to each person with grace and wisdom and making the most of the opportunity. Now my mission statement was getting specific and beginning to take shape. The specific results of my efforts would be if others were drawn toward Jesus. This would be the "noses" that would affirm my mission statement was on target.

Write down some specifics you could include in your statement.

**IT MUST BE SHORT ENOUGH TO BE MEMORIZED.** Here I hit a problem. My original mission statement was too wordy, too difficult to memorize and share with others. Strive to keep yours short enough to memorize but weighty enough to serve a lifetime. As a friend once lamented over her physical size, "I'm just too short for my weight." So think of your mission statement this way: "It needs to be a little short for its weight."

**IT MUST BE WRITTEN DOWN.** Now you're on your way. Write down the responses to these criteria on a large card, and put it in a high profile place like on a bathroom counter or over the kitchen sink. Review, refine, and rewrite until it can last you a lifetime.

My husband and I were having lunch with Larry and Judy Roberts after church one Sunday. As we were discussing mission statements, Larry shared his: "To know God and to make Him known." My heart leapt within me. That's what my mission statement is all about. That's my heart-cry! I immediately adopted it as my concise, easy-to-memorize, mission statement: "To know Jesus Christ and to make Him known." When I later discovered this was similar to the Navigators' mission statement, I knew I was in good company.

Once a soldier understands his mission, he then commits wholeheartedly to it. We're part of a mighty army, and we're on a mission to witness for Jesus Christ. Along the way we will meet the enemy. We should easily recognize him; he's the exact opposite of Jesus.

## Learn to Recognize the Enemy

Lee Alton, a retired colonel in the air force, and his wife, Terry, are tender warriors for Christ. They are warm and personable, yet mighty in the strength of the Lord.

While they were still in the air force, they were moved to Rhode Island. There they quickly got involved in the Officers' Christian Fellowship Bible study. In the group was John, one of Lee's former classmates from the Air Force Academy. John was married to a Thai woman named Mai, a shy, quiet person who was hostile toward Christianity. When John finally decided to get serious about his decision for Christ, he began praying diligently on her behalf.

Terry recounts the story. "We decided to hold the Bible study in a different couple's home every week so that Mai would be there at least once in a while. But none of us wanted to go to their home. It was oppressive and morose and decorated with pictures of Buddha and small Buddhist figurines all over the house.

"You know how every step is an effort when you're trying to walk in a deep pool of water? That's how it felt to walk into that house. You could feel the resistance, the sense of heaviness, the presence of spiritual warfare.

"One evening after the Bible study in their home as Mai and I sat in the living room talking, she started pouring out the story of her childhood. I could hardly believe my ears as she told how her family had betrayed her time and time again.

"Mai had an older sister involved in a prostitution ring. The sister and some of her fellow workers kidnapped Mai, gagged her, tied her up, stuck her in the back of a van, and carted her off to sell into sexual slavery. When at one point they parked the van and everyone got out, Mai was able to untie herself and escape.

"However, a frightening legacy followed her. Unseen chains bound her. Her uncle, who was deeply involved in witchcraft, had claimed Mai for Satan at her birth. She was to be the family member to carry on the uncle's work. As she told me this, the hair on the back of my neck stood straight up, my heart beat out of my chest, and even my feet started to sweat!

"Her uncle had given her some small bottles with human fetuses inside as part of the paraphernalia for their rituals. He told her she had to safeguard these with her life since he had claimed her for Satan's work at birth. She took it seriously; she knew no different.

"She said, 'I feel like I'm in battle, in a war. I'm so tired when I get up in the morning I can hardly function. When I lie in bed, this gold cross John gave me for Christmas burns my skin, and I have to get up and take it off.' We all knew she was not feeling well but had no idea why. Now it began to make sense. I spoke to her about spiritual warfare and how Jesus died for her sins, that He loved her with an unconditional love and desired to claim her as his own, but because her uncle had dedicated her to Satan, the evil one tried to claim her and didn't want her to give her life to Jesus Christ.

"'That's why you're so exhausted when you wake up in the morning,' I told her. 'You literally are in a battle, a spiritual battle, a battle for your soul. Satan does not want you to wear that cross because it's a symbol of Christ's death for your sins. It's a symbol of Jesus' unconditional love for you. Satan doesn't want you to be reminded of this.'

"She hadn't heard that Satan was a murderer, destroyer, and deceiver, or that Jesus called him the father of lies. She was surprised to learn Satan hated her and was out to work evil in her in any way he could. Like many Satan worshipers, she thought he was on her side.

"Just then Lee walked into the room, and I gave him a thumbnail sketch of what had transpired. Mai's husband didn't even know she possessed that horrible paraphernalia. Lee talked to him about taking the authority in the home and how he needed to pray for her and their boys.

"'Mai,' Lee said, 'have you received Jesus Christ as your personal Savior?' Surprisingly enough she said, 'Yes.' But Lee wanted to be sure, considering what he had just heard. So he suggested we all pray right then, and he led Mai in a prayer of salvation.

"As we prayed and rebuked Satan, the most amazing thing occurred: we could actually feel the demonic presence leave that home. I've never been in such a situation, before or since, where I felt the presence of evil so strongly and just as strongly felt it leave. We walked through the entire house and prayed in all the rooms. We shall never forget this time in our lives, for it was truly phenomenal to witness the power of the Lord. Mai's whole countenance was transformed that evening.

"There was an incredible change in Mai's life. She was able to sleep nights and wear her cross. She disposed of the pictures of

Buddha and the small jars of human fetuses, along with every-thing else that was not of God. Christ had broken the hideous legacy left for her. She was a free woman in Christ and became on fire for the Lord."

Lee and Terry, as soldiers of the cross, understood their mission and were armed for battle against the enemy. As soldiers of Christ, we also will be called to do serious battle with the enemy. If we live on our own strength and adequacy, we will surely fail in the spiritual battles. But God has given us the power to fight the spiritual battle in Christ's name.

Let us never be complacent about the spiritual struggle we daily face. It's a real battle for our own souls and the souls of others. But take heart. God and Satan are not two equal forces opposing one another. Satan doesn't move unless God says, "Move." Satan says, "How far?" God says, "Stop here." Satan stops. Satan is allowed to test us, to shake us, to see what we're depending on, but God is always in control. And Jesus has already declared victory.

## It's War

As soldiers of Christ we have three enemies: the world, the flesh, and the devil. We need to keep in mind that all of these enemies are at work in the life of an unsaved person. The world—this present world system apart from God—is chaotic, bent on its own destruction. We have enough atomic power in the world to destroy the entire human race and enough moral decay to self-destruct. Nonbelievers will most likely be quite attached to the world and embrace its values. Whatever feels good is the guiding principle. We shouldn't expect them to see it destructiveness because they don't have the mind of Christ.

The flesh is a relentless enemy which cries out, "I can do it. I'm adequate. I'm smart, powerful, and self-sufficient." When we sin, sometimes we give Satan more credit than he is due. We say, "The devil made me do it." But often it is human desire and self-will, which is weak, vulnerable, and undisciplined. Our human nature says, "I want what I want when I want it." Nonbelievers usually see no problem with that, and we need to understand how they think.

Then there is the great enemy, Satan. He lies, deceives, tempts, accuses, and destroys. He uses humans to oppose God's work, and he attempts to defeat believers. However, "the one [Jesus] who is in you is greater than the one [Satan] who is in the world" (1 John 4:4). Satan is greater than we are but not greater than Christ in us. We have One who is all powerful, all knowing, and ever present, living in the hearts of believers. He is the Victor!

If we could see the spiritual world, I'm sure we would be overwhelmed. *This Present Darkness,* a novel by Frank E. Peretti, gives much insight into spiritual warfare and the necessity of prayer. He vividly describes a fictitious demon: "Its leering, bulbous eyes reflected the stark blue light of the full moon with their own jaundiced glow. The gnarled head protruded from hunched shoulders, and wisps of rancid red breath seethed in labored hisses through rows of jagged fangs. From its crawling posture it reared up on its legs and looked about the quiet neighborhood, the black, leathery jowls pulling back into a hideous death-mask grin."[1]

Whether that's an accurate description of a demon or not, I must say the book did a great deal for my prayer life regarding spiritual warfare. Of course Peretti's story is imaginary and is not meant to be a study in the doctrine of angels or prayer, but it has stirred many believers to get on their knees. My husband has met a number of men reading Peretti's book while traveling on airplanes. Several were nonbelievers for whom it aroused a sincere interest in Jesus Christ. It's amazing what God will use. It could be one of the tools God uses in the life of an unsaved person you are praying for. Read it first. It may be just what your friend needs to read. Or it may be just for you.

We are to be aware of the schemes of Satan but not have an unhealthy interest in him—just a biblical one. In the military the intelligence corps enables the soldiers to identify and understand the enemy. Likewise, throughout the Scriptures, God tells us who the enemy is, where he is, and what he is capable of doing. No excuse for being caught off guard.

We are so easily tempted to think our enemies are human, and so we try to use worldly weapons. They are useless against the evil spiritual forces as they seek to control the minds and lives of believers and nonbelievers. In Ephesians 6:11–13 believers are told: "Put on the full armor of God so that you can take your stand against the devil's schemes. For our struggle is not against flesh and blood, but against the rulers, against the authorities, against the powers of this dark world and against the spiritual forces of evil in the heavenly realms. Therefore put on the full armor of God, so that when the day of evil comes, you may be able to *stand* your ground, and after you have done everything, to *stand*" (italics mine).

Note that nowhere in these verses are believers urged to attack and advance. The key to this section is *stand*. As pilgrims we are to walk, as disciples we are to baptize and teach, as witnesses we are to journey to the ends of the earth, as athletes we are to run, as branches we are to abide, as eagles we are to soar, and as sheep we are listen to our Shepherd's voice. But as soldiers we are to stand firm, not giving up ground and not retreating. Satan is the one who makes the attack.

## Standing Firm

Ann and her husband, Al, a retired veterinarian, live on a ranch in Carefree, Arizona. Ann has always enjoyed being surrounded by animals, as evidenced by their small zoo on the ranch, which houses a wallaby, many exotic birds, three lamas, several lemurs, a number of mules, and a potbellied pig named Sophie, who adores Fig Newtons.

Ann was trying to enjoy a wonderfully warm spring day in the desert. All would have been perfect had she not been nursing a broken ankle. Ann said, "This particular day my foot began to throb, so I went into the living room to elevate it.

"As I hobbled into the living room, Joanne, our resident 'hunting cat,' was in her hunting mode. She loves to stalk rattlesnakes, so that was not a good sign. That's when I heard it— the unmistakable staccato rattle of a ticked-off, highly poisonous, just out of hibernation, ill-humored rattlesnake. Joanne stood absolutely still, staring at a rattlesnake in the middle of my kitchen floor!

"I'm used to capturing rattlesnakes with a snake stick, but it was in the barn, and I couldn't possibly get to it. Besides, I didn't want to take my eyes off the snake, knowing if he slithered under the refrigerator we'd never get him out.

"Then it dawned on me. I had two snake sticks under my arms—my crutches. I had to make the snake strike the stick at least twice to get rid of some of his venom so if he bit me it would not be as severe. I turned one of my crutches upside down and poked him with the rubber end. He struck, then struck again, obviously disappointed that he was unable to paralyze my crutch.

"As the snake headed for the baseboard, I hobbled after him, crutch in hand. Taking great pains not to ruin his fine scaly skin, I finally pinned his head down in a corner with the end of my crutch.

"Now what? I was standing on one leg with a crutch under one arm and the other crutch over a dangerous snake. I was too far away from the knives to kill him. So there I stood, immovable.

"Al was due home in about twenty minutes, but it felt like an eternity before I heard his car coming up the road. When he came into the kitchen, his eyes met mine and he realized, 'Something's wrong.' No kidding! His eyes traveled along my arm, down the crutch, onto the floor, and stopped at the rattler.

"His jaw dropped and he said, 'Hold it there! Don't move!' As if he thought I was going to break into a line dance. Al hurriedly left the room…and came back with the camera for a Kodak moment! People have been imprisoned for less.

"But the story did have a happy ending. Al eventually killed the rattler, and he now serves a very useful purpose as a hatband. The snake that is!"

Ann understands standing firm, holding the enemy at bay. He's still dangerous, still venomous, still angry, but unable to cause harm. Likewise, a soldier of Christ standing firm *spiritually* against the enemy remains immovable against the enemy—by the power of Christ in him.

### Some Battles Are on the Home Front

Kathleen Hall, a special friend of mine, made a decision for Christ in August of 1975 at Winnetka Bible Church. Kathleen says, "My friend Susan was having trouble finding the words to share her faith with me. So she invited me to a vacation Bible school that had a mom's class. I didn't know I was searching for God; I thought I was searching for answers, comfort, and help, especially for my marriage.

"David and I were like two trains on different tracks going in opposite directions. We were selfish and self-centered. I was fighting for my rights and expected David to fulfill every need in my life. At the same time David was trying to get his worth and fulfillment from his business. I was very disappointed with my husband and my marriage. I wanted to change the man, but of course I hadn't thought much about changing me.

"One evening I went over the verses I had been learning about having life and having it more abundantly. That's what I wanted. I knew I needed to make a decision to trust Christ, seek forgiveness for my sins, and pray. So right there at my desk in my kitchen I prayed. It was amazing. I felt physically enveloped by light and warmth. I made my decision the night before the last day of vacation Bible school.

"On our last day of class the pastor of the church said, 'I would like to meet with each one of you who has made that decision this week.' When I went to his office, he asked me, 'What do you think your husband will say about this commitment you've made?' That was easy for me to answer: 'I hadn't planned on telling him.' He gently but firmly said, 'I suggest you go home and tell your husband what you have done. Tell him once and then don't mention it again. Just go home and love him and wait for God to bring him to Himself.'

"Over the years God reminded me many times of the pastor's words. I can honestly say I didn't badger David or nag him. I spoke little of my Christian life. The wisdom of 1 Peter 3:1–2 became my guide: 'Wives, in the same way be submissive to your husbands so that, if any of them do not believe the word, they may be won over without words by the behavior of their wives, when they see the purity and reverence of your lives.' I wanted the quality of my life to win him over.

"But I was desperate to have him become a believer. I had been praying fervently, pleading with God. I was also angry at God for not changing David's behavior. I started to feel God was withholding this from me because I knew He could intervene if He wanted to.

"Then one night as I was praying and crying it was as if God said, 'You're right. I can and I will intervene. But there's some work I want to do in your life. The greater work for the moment is changing you and your heart. I'll worry about David. Let's talk about you.'

"I always wanted to see David change. It never occurred to me that I might need to search my soul and change. So I asked, 'What is it, Lord?' I didn't have to wait very long for an answer. If was as if God said, 'I desire your total surrender to Me. I want your complete devotion, obedience, and submission. I want you to follow me with every ounce of your being. I want all of you.'

"That night through my tears I surrendered all I knew. After that, things started happening so fast it made my head spin. It's as though God said, 'I've been waiting for this, Kathleen.'

"Luis Palau, an internationally known evangelist, was coming to our church. In preparation for his arrival several Bible studies were started for the men. David decided to attend a study. I was so excited I could hardly contain myself.

"When Palau preached and gave the invitation, David literally bolted down the aisle. I had waited years for God to bring David to Himself. But I'm convinced it was prayer, my desire to love and honor him, my surrender to the Lord, and my zipped lip that finally brought him around. Of course I recognize it was the work of the Holy Spirit. I just tried not to get in the way."

Christian soldiers often have unbelieving spouses. What can they do? Stand in the gap. Stand firm in prayer. Be strong and courageous in the Lord. We cannot argue, cajole, scheme, or manipulate anyone into the Kingdom. But we can love, honor, respect, and even praise our spouses exceedingly for their admirable qualities.

A friend of mine angrily remarked, "But he doesn't deserve honor and respect." That may be true. His actions might not be honorable or deserving of respect, but the Bible says in Ephesians 5:33 that wives are to respect their husbands. Not "if he's a great guy" or "when he finally gets his act together." But now, today, love him just the way he is. If we are singing "Oh How I Love Jesus" but refuse to honor and respect our spouses, we are disobeying God. How will we ever win them over if our behavior rebels against the truth of Scripture? Why should the nonbeliever trust Christ whom they cannot see, when the believer standing right in front of them refuses to demonstrate forgiveness and grace?

Someone once said, "Take a good look at your relationship with your husband, and you will have an accurate view of your relationship with the Lord. If you are stubborn, strong willed, unyielding, rebellious, and bitter toward your husband, then you are most likely not truly yielded to Christ." That's a sobering thought. Love those unsaved spouses to the Lord, just as Jesus has loved us to Himself.

## Just-Say-the-Word Soldiers

In Matthew 8:5–13 we read of the centurion who came to Jesus, asking for help. "Lord," he said, "my servant lies at home paralyzed and in terrible suffering." Jesus simply answered him, "I will go and heal him." But the centurion in all humility replied,

"Lord, I do not deserve to have you come under my roof. But just say the word, and my servant will be healed. For I myself am a man under authority, with soldiers under me. I tell this one, 'Go,' and he goes; and that one, 'Come,' and he comes. I say to my servant, 'Do this,' and he does it."

Jesus marveled at his faith when he heard this. But there's more. The centurion also understood power, authority, and submission. He had to answer to those in authority, and his soldiers had to answer to him. Without this kind of discipline and submission there would be chaos in the camp. His faith demonstrated that he knew Jesus had absolute authority over him, his servant, and his servant's paralysis. "Just say the word." That's all he needed—just the word. Oh for a whole unit of men and women who understand lordship, submission, authority, leadership, and faith like this centurion. How the Lord must yearn for such followers.

It's time to ask ourselves, "What kind of soldier am I really? Am I a just-say-the-word soldier? Is Christ the ultimate authority in my life? Or am I guilty of insubordination? If a whole unit had my level of spiritual preparedness, how would we affect the enemy? What threat would we pose?" God can't use insubordinate soldiers, but He will use, honor, bless, reward, and do powerful feats in the lives of just-say-the-word soldiers.

Right now, this moment, offer whatever you're holding back—your life, your gifts, yourself—to the Lord. Tell Him what He is longing to hear from you, "Lord, just say the word, and I will do it. I want to be a just-say-the-word soldier."

## HOOKS TO HANG YOUR HAT ON

• Remember you're on a mission from God.
Ask Him to show you how He wishes to accomplish
this through you.

• Ask yourself, "Why am I doing this? What is my big purpose?"

• A mission statement is a clear, concise statement
of your life's purpose in the light of witnessing for Christ
and your reason for being.

• Without submitting our daily decisions to a mission statement
we could be at the mercy of the tyranny of the moment.

• Review, study, and develop your spiritual gifts.

• Be able to give at least five "identities" of a believer
if a nonbeliever asked you what it means to be a Christian.
See the list at the end of this chapter.

• Begin work on your mission statement today
by searching the Scriptures for verses God uses to speak to you
about your purpose.

• Measure your progress by how you manifest the fruit
of the Spirit today as compared to last year.
Are you more patient, kind, gentle?

• Make plans as big as the ones God has for you.

## ALL THINGS CONSIDERED

1. What practical way might your life indicate you are on a mission from God? What impact has your mission produced?

2. How would you define Moses' mission statement? Esther's? Paul's?

3. List your spiritual gifts. What are you doing to develop them? What else could you be doing?

4. Take five "identities" from the end of this chapter, look up the verses, and describe what each personally means to you.

5. Find two or more Scripture verses that begin to define your "big purpose" in life. Combine them into one sentence.

6. Write down two realistic goals you believe God has for your life. Are they long range? Will these goals challenge you for a lifetime? Can you measure them daily? Make them specific and short. Write out a more complete mission statement using your Scripture verses and these questions. Now make it a little short for its weight. Condense it.

7. Can you think of a time when following Jesus Christ just seemed too difficult? What kept you going? Commitment? Act of the will? Love for Christ? How could this encourage a non-believer you are witnessing to?

8. Have you ever found yourself "standing firm" against the enemy? What happened? What kept you standing? What weapons did you use? How can this help you in witnessing to nonbelievers?

9. Reread 1 Peter 3:1–2. Using a dictionary, define the word submissive. Does this mean wives should be doormats? How can one be submissive and still have dignity and worth? Give three examples of submissiveness in life other than in marriage. How can we demonstrate purity and reverence in our lives as witnesses of Christ? Give two examples.

10. How will the message of this chapter equip you to be a better witness for Jesus Christ?

## How God Sees Believers

| | |
|---|---|
| Ambassadors | 2 Corinthians 5:20 |
| Blameless | Colossians 1:22 |
| Branches | John 15:5 |
| Bride of Christ | Ephesians 5:25–27, 32 |
| Brothers of Jesus | Hebrews 2:11 |
| Called by His Name | Isaiah 43:7 |
| Children of God | 1 John 3:1; Romans 8:15–16 |
| Chosen Ones | John 15:16 |
| Citizens of Heaven | Philippians 3:20 |
| Complete | Colossians 2:10 |
| Earthen Vessels | 2 Corinthians 4:7 |
| Elect | Mark 13:27 |
| Faith-Walking People | 2 Corinthians 5:7 |
| Fellow Workers | 1 Corinthians 3:9 |
| Fragrance of Christ | 2 Corinthians 2:14–16 |
| Friends of Jesus | John 15:13–15 |
| Free | Romans 6:18; 8:2; Galatians 5:1 |
| Forgiven | Colossians 3:13; 1 John 1:9; Acts 10:43 |
| Gift | John 17:6 |
| God's Workmanship | Ephesians 2:10 |
| Heirs | Romans 8:17 |
| Holy | Colossians 1:22 |
| Honored | Psalm 91:15 |
| Image Bearers | Genesis 1:26 |
| Light of the World | Matthew 5:14 |
| Living Stones | 1 Peter 2:5 |
| Loved | John 17:23 |

| | |
|---|---|
| More than Conquerors | Romans 8:37 |
| New Creation | 2 Corinthians 5:17 |
| Partakers of the Divine Nature | 2 Peter 1:4 |
| Peacemakers | Matthew 5:9; Romans 12:18 |
| Precious in God's Sight | Isaiah 43:4 |
| Reconcilers | 2 Corinthians 5:18 |
| Redeemed | Ephesians 1:7 |
| Regenerated, Renewed | Titus 3:5 |
| Royal Priesthood | 1 Peter 2:5, 9 |
| Runners in a Race | Hebrews 12:1–3 |
| Saints | Philippians 1:1; 4:21, 22; Romans 1:7 |
| Salt of the Earth | Matthew 5:13 |
| Saved | Romans 10:9, 10 |
| Servants of Christ | Galatians 1:10 |
| Sheep | John 10:14–15 |
| Soldiers | 2 Timothy 2:3 |
| Temples of the Holy Spirit | 1 Corinthians 3:16; 6:19 |
| Witnesses | Acts 1:8 |

# CHAPTER EIGHT

# THE URGENT BUSINESS OF BELIEVERS

*Be merciful to those who doubt; snatch others from the fire and save them.*

JUDE 22–23

I n some circumstances there is not time to plant the seed of the Word of God and watch it grow, or to wait with the patience and perseverance of a fisher of men. At these times we must seize the moment and snatch others from the fire because the truth is, the lost are facing a Christless eternity in hell, in the unquenchable fire.

Have you noticed how no one ever wants to talk about hell? Little wonder. It's a place "where their worm does not die, and the fire is not quenched" (Mark 9:48). The wicked will be cast into "the fiery furnace, where there will be weeping and gnashing of teeth" (Matthew 13:50). "Their place will be in the fiery lake of burning sulfur" (Revelation 21:8). Not exactly dinner conversation.

It's difficult even to imagine a place where the inhabitants are consumed with hate, anger, greed, wickedness, bitterness, selfishness, debauchery, and every kind of utter decay and rottenness of spirit for all eternity. Hell is forever devoid of God and goodness, joy and peace, patience and kindness. And that's where our unbelieving neighbor, relative, friend, coworker, golfing buddy, tennis partner, or the stranger on the street is traveling toward.

I used to be lighthearted about hell before I believed in Christ. In fact, I remember laughingly telling a friend of mine as we were discussing the heat of hell, "So how hot can they make the coals? Give me a break; how hot can it be? Hotter than Chicago in August? I doubt it!" I had no understanding. I had no fear. I had no relationship with Jesus. I wasn't aware of the awful truth regarding such a serious matter.

Hell is no mythical place. "The knowledge of hell comes almost exclusively from the teachings of Christ, who spoke on the doctrine of hell clearly and emphatically on a number of occasions. The Bible does not give the physical location of hell or anything about its furnishings, but it assures readers that those whose sins are not atoned for by Jesus Christ will receive perfect justice from God, that they will receive exactly what they deserve for all eternity, which will be a most miserable fate. This ought to be one of the impelling motives making evangelism the urgent business of all Christians."[1]

No matter how "together" nonbelievers appear to be, no matter how handsome or lovely the exterior, no matter how honest or kind, no matter how good or loving, hell is their final destination. Will we be the ones to help escort them to safety? Will we be a part of the rescue team that points the way to eternal safety? Will we say on bended knees, "Count me in, Lord. I'm available, I'm ready, send me"?

## The Littlest Angel

A friend of mine, John Politan, tells this story of Albie Pearson, who had an opportunity to seize the moment. Albie was a baseball player for the Los Angeles Angels when they were first added as an expansion team to the American League. Albie, a Christian, was considered a "religious" kind of guy in baseball circles, and being the shortest man in baseball at the time, at about 5'5", he was appropriately dubbed the "littlest angel."

In 1961 the Southern California March of Dimes Foundation chose two people to cochair the fund drive for that year—Marilyn Monroe from the entertainment field and Albie Pearson from the sports world. While their pictures appeared together on posters and advertisements, they never met until the campaign wound to a close. Near the end of the baseball season a special pregame award ceremony was slated to thank both celebrities for their support of the March of Dimes.

Pearson said, "I arrived at the ballpark early after having a disagreement with my wife. Quite frankly that was nothing new. At that time in my life I was having disagreements with everyone and everything. I was disgruntled with life, and although I was a born-again Christian, I had been out of fellowship with God for some time. I had cut off my connection to Jesus Christ. I wasn't having daily devotions, spending time in the Word, or walking in obedience. I wasn't even considering the cause of Christ, let alone witnessing for Him.

"When I arrived that evening an hour and half before game time, the dugout was empty and few people were in the stands. It was eerie. There was none of the usual hustle and bustle. Then lo and behold, who should walk into the dugout all alone but Marilyn Monroe!

"As my eyes first met hers, I was stunned. She was a stark contrast to the woman I had seen in the movies, posters, papers, and television. She had a cold, gloomy pallor and a gray, somber expression. Her eyes told a story of longing and emptiness that was absolutely compelling. Here was this blonde bombshell, this famous star that men worshiped and women envied. Yet all I saw was despair, loneliness, and sadness through and through.

"Then I thought I heard something rather strange. I faintly recognized it as that 'still small voice' in the back of my head saying to me, 'This woman is lonely, lost, and in need of Christ. Share the gospel with her.' But I had been out of fellowship for such a long time that I totally resisted the urge. Only God knew how long it had been since I had sought His presence; I'd forgotten. Miss Monroe and I had just started to chat briefly when we were interrupted by the photographers, press, and public relations people walking into the dugout.

"When the awards ceremony began at home plate, the most incredible metamorphosis took place before my eyes. The house lights went on, and the announcement began: 'Introducing Marilyn Monroe, the star of stage, screen, and TV!' As she started up the dugout steps, she hiked up her skirt a few inches and wiggled her way to the stand. All the while she was laughing, waving at the wolf whistles, and blowing kisses to the crowd. She had painted on her theatrical face, plastered a fake smile over the anguished one, and lit up for the excited crowd. She did her 'Marilyn Monroe impersonation.'

"The entire time the awards were given and dignitaries were speaking that 'still small voice' of God continued to urge me to speak to her about Jesus. I was thinking, 'She needs to know Christ. Share the gospel with her. She needs to know Christ. Share the gospel with her.' And the entire time I kept resisting it. 'Oh that's crazy, I'm not going to do that. That's Marilyn Monroe!' I kept telling myself.

"As the awards ceremony was over and we were walking off the field, I found myself directly behind her. Just as we got to the edge of the dugout steps, she whirled around and stared me right in the face and said, 'You want to tell me something. What is it?' I looked back at her stupefied as she stood waiting with that yearning in her face. I knew God was compelling me to share the gospel, yet I resisted again. I stuttered and stammered and said, 'Well,…uh no, I don't know what…uh you're talking about. I don't want to tell you anything.' She looked at me quizzically and said, 'Well okay, but I still feel you have something to say to me.' Then she turned and went down into the dugout.

"Later on I saw her in the eighth row with Joe DiMaggio. During the fifth or sixth inning they walked out. That was the last time I saw Marilyn Monroe. Although I felt some remorse about not acting on the prompting of the Holy Spirit, I figured I'd get over it.

"A few days later my wife awakened me by throwing a copy of the *L. A. Times* on my bed. The headlines read 'Marilyn Monroe Dead of Drug Overdose at the Age of 41.' In horror I read the account and reflected on just the other night when I had refused to share the gospel with her. Tears welled up in my eyes and I sobbed uncontrollably. I climbed out of my bed and immediately went to my knees. I begged God to please, please forgive me and restore me to a right relationship with Him. I made a vow that if God in His infinite grace and mercy would ever give me the privilege to share the gospel of Jesus Christ with anyone else for the rest of my life, I wouldn't fail to seize the moment. I wouldn't blow it. I would be ready to give an answer for the hope that is within me. I got my heart right with God that morning and vowed never to let go of it again."

## Another Opportunity, Another Ending

But the story doesn't actually end there. Brenda Desmaris is a dear friend of mine who truly desires to be obedient. However, like many of us, she is also a bit reluctant at times.

Her Uncle Tooley had a special place in her heart, so when he showed up in town one day she was delighted. But his wife had separated from him, and he was in a deep depression he couldn't shake. He still loved his wife and found life meaningless and empty without her. What troubled Brenda even more was that her uncle didn't have a personal relationship with Jesus. His life was indeed without meaning.

After he told Brenda the pain he felt over his broken marriage, Brenda told him of some hard times she had gone through with her husband. When he asked, "How did you get through it? How did you do it?" she wanted to give him the gospel and tell him about Jesus, her source of hope, but she didn't. Instead she said, "Well, I just somehow got through it."

Haven't many of us done that? It isn't that our hearts are

rebellious or that we've cut ourselves off from Jesus, but perhaps we think, "I'll wait till next time. I'm fearful he'll reject me. He'll think I'm foolish...or a fanatic. Next time will be soon enough. Next time he'll be ready to hear...or I'll be ready to talk."

A few days later I shared the story of Albie Pearson and Marilyn Monroe with Brenda. After I left, Brenda was convicted of not having shared Jesus with her uncle. She thought, "What if Uncle Tooley died and I never shared the gospel with him?" Brenda then prayed, "Oh Lord, give me another chance. I will not fail You. I will tell him about You, Jesus. I'll tell him what You did for me, my husband, and our family."

Another chance came a week later. Uncle Tooley asked the very same question again. Brenda then shared with him openly, simply, and freely what Christ had done in her life and what Jesus could do for him. With a sense of urgency she invited him to church. Shortly after that evening Uncle Tooley went forward and trusted Jesus with his eternal destiny.

He was a baby Christian. Just beginning to learn God's ways. Just starting to open his heart to God's truths. Just seeking to understand God's commands. Then the news came like a sword through Brenda's heart. Her Uncle Tooley had committed suicide. Brenda cried out, "I don't understand. How could he do this? He was a Christian!"

I searched for words of comfort. I carefully considered how I could reply and said, "Brenda, I can't help but feel how gracious the Lord was to reveal Himself to Uncle Tooley before he died. Our all-knowing God saw into the future and knew he would commit suicide. We know this was not God's plan, but Uncle

Tooley had free will. Jesus loved him so much He couldn't bear to spend eternity without him. So He revealed Himself to your uncle when he desperately needed Him. He used you to help rescue him from the fiery inferno."

Two stories, both ending in suicide. The difference? One nonbeliever didn't hear the gospel when she needed it most. The other heard and responded. We cannot see into the future; we cannot hope to know another's hidden thoughts. But we can respond to the universal need of every man, woman, and child—the need for a personal relationship with Jesus Christ. Sharing the message of Christ is a matter of life and death.

## Rescuers of the Lost Stay Connected to Christ

We cannot share, however, unless the message of Christ dwells in our hearts. My professor at Phoenix Seminary, Kem Oberholtzer, recently had our class commit John 15:1–17 to memory. What a wonderful exercise! This chapter compares abiding in Christ to the relationship of a vine and its branches. Jesus says, "I am the vine; you are the branches. If a man remains in me and I in him, he will bear much fruit; apart from me you can do nothing" (15:5). Basically the verse says if we are not connected to Jesus, our lifeline, we can do nothing of eternal value.

We could be filled with biblical knowledge, attend church regularly, sing in the choir, teach Sunday school, or give to the poor. But if we're not hooked up to the lifeline of the Vine, if we're not abiding in Christ, we won't be prepared to seize the moment.

## Hide the Word of God in Your Heart

Abiding, dwelling, living in, being connected to Christ is to be prepared for whatever God has planned for us. One of the best ways to abide in Christ is to commit Bible verses to memory.

Is the Word of God fresh on our lips and tongues? Have we this day tasted its sweetness for ourselves? We cannot give out that which we do not have. We cannot lead the lost out of their darkness without first holding up the light. Today, this moment, purpose in your heart to begin to memorize scripture. You might begin with John 15:5 or John 15:13 or even John 15:1–17.

I've always loved the Gospel of John, so one day I decided to memorize the first eighteen verses and see what I could do from there. Those verses are packed with the person of Jesus Christ. Since then I've had many opportunities to tell nonbelievers what I have in my heart when they ask, "Who is Jesus Christ?" This has been a great tool for witnessing.

I tell them from John 1:1–18 that Jesus is the Word, He was with God in the beginning (eternal), He was God (the Almighty), through Him all things were made (Creator), in Him was life (Life-Giver), and that life was the light of men (Light-Giver). The light shines in the darkness. The true light that gives light to every person came into the world (Light of the World). To all who received Him and believed in His name, He gave the right to become children of God. He is full of grace and truth, and He has explained God because He has seen Him. All this and much more comes just from John 1:1–18. Some nonbelievers are put off if we quote verses to them, but we can confidently share the truth of the Word in natural conversation rather than by recitation if we have hidden it in our hearts.

I remember one individual who was astounded to learn that Jesus was eternal (John 1:1). He thought Jesus was first created when He was born of Mary. "If He's eternal, maybe He really is God. If He's really God, maybe I should trust Him with my eternal destiny." (That's the shortened version of his search that led him to trust Christ.)

One woman I witnessed to was totally fascinated by the fact that Jesus was Creator (John 1:3). She wanted to know more because she began to see Him as all powerful. "What else did He do? What can He do for me?" Yet another woman had never heard that she needed to believe in what Jesus did on the cross (John 1:12). She received and believed and became a child of God. They all were drawn into God's saving arms by first hearing the Word of God. The Word brings light to those who walk in darkness. "Your word is a lamp to my feet and a light for my path" (Psalm 119:105). Bear the light in this dark world.

Jesus did all the real work, but He uses us to help bring the lost to safety. In a sense we are on a rescue mission to help snatch the lost from the fires of hell. The problem is that some of us say "save" is good but "saving" is too hard. Add the "ing" and we run, especially if it means immediate action. My hope and prayer is that your heart is stirred to action and that you have a sense of urgency for those headed for a fiery destruction. Wouldn't you agree that sharing the gospel is indeed the urgent business of believers?

---
### HOOKS TO HANG YOUR HAT ON
---

• Pray today for your party of three.

• Our good and kind but unbelieving friends
are facing a Christless eternity, heading straight into hell,
into the unquenchable fire.
We may be called upon to help rescue them.
Remember where they are headed. How are you prepared?

• Hang onto the Vine.
When we've depleted our own limited resources, we will always
have the unlimited resources of God.

• Abide in Him. Memorize John 15:5; it will serve you well.

• If you really want a challenge, begin memorizing John 1:1–18
or John 15:1–17.
You'll be well equipped if you do.

---
### ALL THINGS CONSIDERED
---

1. How ready and prepared are you to share the gospel with a nonbeliever? How could you train to improve that? When will you begin?

2. Let's examine three ways to train for the "rescue."

"Do your best to present yourself to God as one approved, a workman who does not need to be ashamed and who correctly handles the word of truth" (2 Timothy 2:15). How will you present yourself as an approved workman to God?

"Pray also for me, that whenever I open my mouth, words may be given me so that I will fearlessly make known the mystery of the gospel, for which I am an ambassador in chains. Pray that I may declare it fearlessly, as I should" (Ephesians 6:19–20). Rewrite and personalize this prayer to boldly share the gospel. Commit it to daily prayer.

"We have different gifts, according to the grace given us. If a man's gift is prophesying, let him use it in proportion to his faith. If it is serving, let him serve; if it is teaching, let him teach; if it is encouraging, let him encourage; if it is contributing to the needs of others, let him give generously; if it is leadership, let him govern diligently; if it is showing mercy, let him do it cheerfully" (Romans 12:6–8). Do you know your spiritual gifts? What are you doing to develop them? How are you using them at this time? Why would this help in our training for the rescue of our "three most wanted"?

3. "I have hidden your word in my heart" (Psalm 119:11). Discuss how Scripture memorization will help us in the rescue.

4. Share a time when you experienced the transforming power of prayer. Were you the one who prayed? Were you the beneficiary of another's prayer? Or were you an observer of the results of someone else's heartfelt prayer?

5. "For nothing is impossible with God" (Luke 1:37). Are you praying for someone who is seemingly an impossible case for salvation? Why then do you continue praying?

6. "This is the confidence we have in approaching God: that if we ask anything according to his will, he hears us. And if we know that he hears us—whatever we ask—we know that we have what we asked of him" (1 John 5:14–15). What must we have in approaching God? How are we to pray? What will He do? What about the free will of the ones we are praying for who are bent on destruction? Will God override a person's free will? Should we ever stop praying for them?

7. Have you ever dropped your connection to God? Share your experience.

8. When we've depleted our limited resources, we will always have the unlimited resources of God. What personal resources do you sometimes find yourself depending upon? How do we depend on or tap into the unlimited resources of God?

# CHAPTER NINE

# DREAM BIG DREAMS FOR GOD

*Now to him who is able to do immeasurably more than all we ask or imagine, according to his power that is at work within us, to him be glory in the church and in Christ Jesus throughout all generations, for ever and ever! Amen.*

EPHESIANS 3:20–21

She was just a little nun named Teresa, but her dreams were extravagant enough that heaven took notice. The world hadn't heard of her yet, and *Time* magazine certainly wasn't considering her for their cover, but the God of the universe knew her intimately and heard from her frequently. She had most likely appeared on the cover of *Heavenly Times* magazine read by all the saints and angels—"Teresa Dreaming Big Dreams Again."

Teresa went to her superiors one day and said, "I've got three pennies and a dream from God to build an orphanage."

They looked at each other in disbelief and responded, "Teresa, you can't build an orphanage with three pennies. With three pennies you can do nothing."

She smiled and said, "Oh I know that, but with three pennies and a dream from God I can do anything."

Mother Teresa knew something that precious few dare

imagine. If God puts a dream in your heart, He will accomplish it. She relied on the fact God would equip her and empower her to achieve this outrageous aspiration. Today Mother Teresa has appeared before presidents, royalty, and heads of state. She has been featured in *Time* and a host of publications. The world knows of this tiny woman's dream and of Jesus, in whose name it has all been done. When God wants something important accomplished, He takes a dream and plants it in a willing heart. Then He works, waits, and watches.

## *Reluctant to Fulfill God's Dream?*

The eyes of the Lord search the earth for willing hearts to fulfill His dream—that all might come to a saving knowledge of Jesus Christ. However, He often finds believers reluctant to carry the message. Such a person was Moses.

Moses lived forty years in Pharaoh's household being a "somebody." Then he lived forty years as a shepherd being a "nobody." Another forty years were spent in the wilderness contending with the Israelites learning how God could take a "nobody" and make him a "somebody for God." The Lord has a way of bursting into the ordinary and making it extraordinary, of taking a life and creating a living testimony to His glory.

Moses had tried by his own hand to free the Hebrews. Perhaps the hope of liberating God's people had been conceived in Moses' heart as a young man. He may have thought, "I have big dreams. I'll watch for just the right moment and circumstances." Then one day he saw an Egyptian beating one of the Hebrews. Moses killed the Egyptian, buried him in the sand, and then had to flee from Pharaoh. Moses' plan wasn't God's idea. We can dream a big dream for God, but if He isn't the One who places it within us, it could be a real nightmare.

After fleeing Egypt, Moses became a shepherd in the land of Midian. He didn't exactly have the time of his life tending flocks for his father-in-law, but it was a living. One day while watching the flocks, Moses was confronted with a burning bush. "A burning bush that isn't consumed? This deserves a closer look." But a burning bush wasn't the only thing God did to gain Moses' attention. God called Moses by name: "Moses! Moses!" Moses answered, "Here I am." That phrase in Hebrew literally means "behold me" and generally expresses a readiness to obey.

Have you heard God call you by name? I have. It is a fearsome and awesome thing when you know it is the Lord's voice echoing in your heart. God has great dreams for us. How He must long to hear us respond, "Behold me." Oh, that our reply would always be "Here I am."

Be assured, God always calls us to greatness, not greatness as the world defines it but greatness in His eyes. And if it's God's wonderful plan for us, why do we hesitate to do the things that are great in His eyes? Could one reason be that it doesn't look so great to us? Witness to the homeless, the dying, my unfriendly neighbor, my Jewish friend, my atheist brother-in-law? Lord, I don't think so.

The truth of the matter is we're not much different than Moses. His first words to the Lord were "Here I am." But that was before he heard what he was here for. Then Moses revealed his true nature by reluctantly responding to God's summons, saying, "It's too hard. The people will never believe me." Does that sound like a familiar excuse for not witnessing? Moses also told God he was "slow of speech and tongue." He was actually complaining of not being quick-witted enough, but he sure was quick with an excuse!

When God puts big dreams in the hearts of devoted followers, He says, "It's not you doing something *for* Me, but rather I am going to do something *through* you." The issue is not what we are capable of, but rather what He is capable of doing through us.

Moses further complained that he didn't even know God's name. What would he tell the people when they asked? God replied, "I AM WHO I AM." God was saying not only was He the God of the past—the God of Abraham, Isaac, and Jacob—but the God of future generations. He further revealed Himself as the God of the present moment. "I am" encompasses all that He is. God proclaimed in His name that He was all Moses would ever need for the tasks he was called to perform.

And He is all we will ever need in the witnessing circumstances of our lives. Why do we fear? Why are we reluctant to share Christ? Have we forgotten Whom we are to depend on? God let Moses know that "I AM" was going to accomplish great things through him. And for us today it is no different. Read this wonderful description of the great "I AM" from Alexander Maclaren: "God lives forevermore, a flame that does not burn out; therefore His resources are inexhaustible. His power unwearied. He needs no rest for recuperation of wasted energy. His gifts diminish not the store which He has to bestow. He gives and is none the poorer. He works and is never weary. He operates unspent; He loves and He loves forever. And through the ages, the fire burns on, unconsumed and undecayed."[1]

This is our great God in whom our faith is to rest. His awesome deeds of the past encourage us to trust Him to fulfill our future dreams. In our human understanding we think our Jewish friend will never come to know Jesus, our unfriendly neighbor is an impossible case, and we've just about given up on our atheistic brother-in-law. Let us recall some of our God's mighty deeds so we may be heartened. "For nothing is impossible with God" (Luke 1:37).

He is the Creator of the universe. The great flood maker. Egyptian plague sender. Bush burner. Red Sea parter. Manna provider. He is the God of Samson's strength, David's anointing, Solomon's wisdom, and Jonah's three-day stay in an underwater hotel.

He is the God of the conception and incarnation of Jesus. The God of the miracle of water becoming wine. The God of water walking, disease healing, dead raising, and sin forgiving. The God of the blood-stained cross. The God of our salvation, justification, sanctification, and resurrection. The God of life everlasting.

This is the God whose desire is for us to go and make disciples, be fishers of men, plant the seed of the Word of God, and rescue the lost from the fires of hell. His power is sufficient to work through us, even the most reluctant of us.

## Never Too Young to Dream for God

The next time you're feeling a bit inadequate for the job, think of Grant Skowron. The Lord has placed great dreams in eight-year-old Grant.

Grant is the son of "Moose" Skowron, a former first baseman for the New York Yankees. Grant was five weeks old when he had his first open heart surgery. For the first two years of his life he was tube fed. He actually didn't eat real food until he was four years old. Imagine, no ice cream, cookies, or hamburgers.

Grant has a pacemaker implanted in his abdomen, which has to be replaced approximately every two years until he is grown. But he takes his condition in stride, in spite of the fact he has already seen the inside of an operating room more times than most of us will in our entire lifetime.

He is like most eight-year-olds, except he dreams big dreams for God. Grant's dream is that all people will come to a personal knowledge of Jesus Christ, and he certainly is doing his share to spread the good news. One day his public school teacher called his parents and said, "I'm afraid Grant is talking about Jesus to absolutely anyone who will listen." His mother replied, "Oh yes, he spreads the J word around a great deal."

And there was the day he went into the school library and firmly but politely asked the librarian, "Why aren't there any books about Jesus in here?" He found it strange that the One who influenced history more than all the armies that ever marched, all the navies that ever sailed, all the parliaments that ever sat, and all the kings who ever reigned was not included in a school library.

I asked Grant how he came to invite Jesus into his heart. He said, "I was sitting in our old house, and I wanted to ask Jesus into my heart because my big brother had and I just knew I was ready. I remember I was eating breakfast and had my Batman costume on. I said, 'Jesus come into my heart, lock the door, throw away the key, and stay in there forever!'"

Though Grant's spiritual heart was healthy, his physical one was not. The Make a Wish Foundation, which was originally set up to grant the fondest wishes of terminally ill children, contacted Sheryl and "Moose" about Grant. Even though he was not considered terminal, his prognosis was unknown, and in such cases the Make a Wish Foundation will often grant a child's wish. The date was set for a man and woman from the foundation to talk with Grant. They interview the children away from their families so the children won't be influenced by the parents, as in "Son, tell them you want to go to Hawaii with your mom and dad."

The interviewers began by asking, "Grant, if you could have anything in the world, what would be your greatest wish?"

"I want to go to heaven and say hi to Jesus," he replied.

"We sure wish we could do that for you, but that's impossible," they responded. "What would be your next best wish?"

"Well then," said the eight-year-old evangelist, "I want *you* to know Jesus, and I want you to go to heaven."

After an hour the couple emerged from the meeting and said, "This child is very concerned about whether we're going to heaven. He was relentless. He insisted we invite Jesus into our hearts. He has to be one of our toughest wish kids."

Grant had a heavenly dream for these people that was far greater than any earthly wish they could grant him. They came to bring happiness and hope to a little boy with a very sick heart, but Grant told them of the One who could bring joy and eternal hope to their needy hearts.

This little guy saw an opportunity and jumped on it. He didn't worry about doctrinal issues. He wasn't concerned that they might think he was weird. He didn't fret over not being able to quote volumes of Scripture. He simply told them if they didn't give their lives to Jesus they could count on going to hell. He is a choleric/high influencer kind of kid!

As adult believers, we are armed with a greater measure of experienced truth than this young man, but are we as eager to share? Would we take the trip to Hawaii and let them find their own way to heaven? Would we have seen this as an opportunity for one of God's dreams to be realized?

## God's Chosen Fast

When God places a dream in our hearts, I strongly believe we should nurture it for a season with prayer but also with fasting. Did I hear an agonized groan and some murmuring from the ranks? Perhaps until now you thought you might go along with some of this, but fasting? "You mean going without food, as in no pizza, tacos, frozen yogurt, or granola?"

Yes, that's exactly what it means. It could mean bread and water or just water. It could mean fasting for three days or one meal. But it almost always means spiritual blessings if done with the proper motivation.

Is your dream to win your neighborhood, your secretary, your friend, your coworker, or loved one for Christ? Has God planted the dream in your heart to write a book on witnessing, teach a Bible study to nonbelievers, become a missionary, distribute Bibles to all the world, or be the best Christian mother, wife, and witness you can be? Are these precious dreams not worth the effort of giving heaven notice of your earnestness by fasting? When we are willing to put aside the appetites of the flesh to seek God, to draw near to Him, to listen for His leading, we are demonstrating to the Lord we mean business.

Isaiah 58:6 says, "Is not this the kind of fasting I have chosen: to loose the chains of injustice and untie the cords of the yoke, to set the oppressed free and break every yoke?" The first thing I noticed about this verse was that God chooses the fast. It is God initiated and God ordained. The Holy Spirit lays a burden upon our hearts and prompts us to respond.

I clearly remember the first time the Lord prompted me to fast. It had to be the Lord because I would never consider skipping a meal on my own accord. I would like to say it was easy, but I approached it with the enthusiasm of having a root canal. What made it bearable was that it was the Holy Spirit's idea, not mine.

It began when two of my friends and I had a short conversation about fasting, over lunch no less. I was remotely interested, but I had always thought fasting was the penalty for exceeding the feed limit. Yet after that conversation it seemed every person I spoke to, every verse I read, every sermon I heard talked about fasting. So the Lord and I started having conversations about this "old spiritual discipline." And He won. He gave me several good reasons, among them some unsaved people in my life, and I felt led to go on a three-day fast, drinking just liquids.

The first morning of the fast I had a doctor's appointment because of digestive problems I had been having. My doctor decided to run a few tests and said, "I would like you to fast for three days just taking liquids, starting today. Do you think you are able to do that?" Was this God's chosen fast, or what?

Even as your eyes fall upon this page, you may be uncomfortably aware that God is speaking to you, and yet you resist, thinking, "Go without eating for spiritual reasons? How could that make a difference?"

Minister and author Andrew Murray wrote, "Fasting helps to express, to deepen, and to confirm the resolution that we are ready to sacrifice anything, to sacrifice ourselves to attain what we seek for the kingdom of God."[2]

Fasting changes minds and hearts, often our own. It is a powerful tool which God has chosen to use throughout the Scriptures and in the lives of people today. It gains His attention and it gains ours. When I fast, I'm amazed how much clearer I think, how much closer I walk with Jesus, and how much stronger I witness.

Fasting isn't exactly a walk in the park. Don't be amazed if you find Satan launching an attack to discourage you from this holy task. Why should we expect anything different than what Jesus faced in His time of fasting before He began His public ministry?

Yet Jesus, in speaking to His disciples about how to fast, said, "When you fast..." (Matthew 6:16–17). The first time I read it, the word when leaped off the page. That must mean Jesus fully expects us to fast. It isn't an option. The only choice is "when" not "if."

I pray that you will watch carefully for the Holy Spirit's leading in your life regarding this discipline. Through fasting we first of all give ourselves to the Lord, and, second, we devote ourselves to securing spiritual ends. Through fasting we can gain a clearer understanding of God's dream for us.

## *I Want to Be Known as a Man of God*

Tom Lehman's dream was to someday win the Masters Golf Tournament. God's dream was that Tom would be a man of God, play golf as a man of God, and tell others how to be a man of God.

To play in the Masters was not an unusual dream for a young man who loved golf and had won his first tournament at eight years old. Tom was a skillful athlete, popular in school, and an excellent student, but at fifteen he felt that everything he was trying to achieve was shallow. None of it gave his life meaning, The more he accomplished, the more depressed he became.

Until he heard of the unconditional love of Jesus Christ. Tom gave his heart to the Lord at a meeting of the Fellowship of Christian Athletes. There he discovered he didn't have to prove himself worthy of love any longer. God loved him no matter what.

Tom says, "It was pretty easy being a Christian in those days. When I attended the University of Minnesota, I was involved in Campus Crusade for Christ and FCA. Being surrounded by Christians at all the retreats, Bible studies, and discipleship meetings gave me a great sense of security and spiritual insulation.

"But I entered a different world when I turned pro at age twenty-three. I simply wasn't prepared to compete against the best golf pros from around the world. Losing all my confidence, I spiraled downhill for the next three years and finally lost my playing rights on the tour.

"Spiritually my life became very difficult too. Until that time I had always depended on the fellowship of other people to keep me uplifted. Now it wasn't there anymore, and I hadn't developed a daily disciplined time in the Bible."

God allowed Tom to experience a few setbacks as he played the small tours in out-of-the-way towns across the country. For a while he lived out of his car with his wife Melissa and their infant daughter in hundred degree weather with a broken air conditioner. He showered in a pouring rain in New Mexico because he couldn't spend the money for a hotel room. With finances from his uncle he traveled to South Africa to play in a tournament only to discover he was ineligible because he had not preregistered. Tom wondered what had happened to his dream. Would it ever be realized? Where was God in all his disappointments?

"It was the Sunday of my first Masters Tournament," says Tom. "I was in fifteenth place going into the last round. Nervous and anxious I sat in the locker room watching Roy Firestone interview Reggie White on ESPN. He asked, 'Reggie, what do you want people to remember you for?' With blazing boldness, yet calm conviction, Reggie said, 'When people think of me, I want them to think of me as a man of God. I want it to be so overpowering and so strong that they'll even forget I played football.' Here was an All Pro, viewed by many as the best defensive lineman who ever played football, saying he wanted to be remembered more as a man of God than a football player. Here was a man of tenderness, yet a man of tremendous strength. I was moved. I was challenged.

"Leaving the locker room that day I gave myself as fully to Christ as I knew how and I prayed, 'Lord, more than anything I want to be known as a man of God.' I went out, shot a sixty-eight, and finished third. The point I was learning is that I had to put my entire focus on being known as a man of God, not as the person who finished first, second, or third.

"Things didn't really start to occur until I surrendered every-thing I knew to God. Then my success opened up more doors to be a witness. People look up to professional athletes, and the more successful you become, the more people want to hear you. I've seen the bottom and the top on the PGA tour. People want to know what happened and how it happened. I tell them about my Lord and Savior, Jesus Christ. I believe God gave me the hard times so that others can better relate to my message. They've had hard times too."

Tom developed a disciplined daily time in the Word. He learned through his dark days the only One to lean on is Christ, that we can't solely depend on other believers to keep us on track. He learned the only way to live, love, and play is to be a man of God. The Lord worked through Tom's dream to fulfill the plans He had for him all along. Between the rain "shower" in 1990 in New Mexico and placing second in his second Masters and attending a presidential state dinner at the White House in 1994, much has happened. God has been hard at work in Tom's life.

Today as Tom travels with his family playing on the tour, he speaks freely of the love of Jesus Christ at churches and dinners and to the media—to anyone who will listen. "God has given me a great responsibility with the success He has granted me," Tom says. "I believe if I don't use this properly He'll choose someone else. I want to be used of God."

### God Will Use Us Right Where We Are

If we are willing, God will often use our dreams to perfect His character in us. God is using Tom in professional golf. God is using Reggie White as an All Pro lineman. God is using Mother Teresa in the streets of Calcutta. God used Moses in the desert. God is using young Grant in his heart disease. And God is using you and me this minute, right where we are in the trials and triumphs of our lives.

God may be using you at the kitchen sink or at your computer terminal, in your Bible study or at the local coffee shop, at the death bed of a loved one or at the birth of a precious child, in a prison cell or in a wheelchair, fly-fishing or planting petunias, shopping at the mall or having a glamour photo, sailing in the Caribbean or grieving at a cemetery, playing baseball or flying in a plane, sitting in the emergency room or having a dinner party. The possibilities are endless and the situations uniquely yours. But God's dream is still the same: to use you to help bring the lost to the One who saves.

Notice the everyday situations in which God has placed you. Open your heart and hands to Him and say, "Here I am. Behold me. I will go for You."

Seize the moment, share the message.

## HOOKS TO HANG YOUR HAT ON

- When God plants the dream in our hearts,
  He is able to accomplish it. Be available.

- We don't do something *for* God.
  God does something *through* us.

- Do at least one practical thing today to help fulfill
  God's dream for you.

- Share your God-given dream with someone
  who will pray for you.

- Think of three things the Israelites had to entrust into
  God's care when facing the Red Sea.
  Entrust one thing, one person, and one set of circumstances
  into God's care today.

- Fast for one meal this week for the purpose
  of spiritual discipline.

- Pray for your party of three during your time of fasting.

- Share one or more of God's character traits (love, faithfulness,
  forgiveness, etc.) with a nonbelieving seeker.
  Tell him or her what your personal experience
  of God's character has been.

## ALL THINGS CONSIDERED

1. What dream has God planted in your heart? Share how God revealed that to you. What practical thing are you doing today to help fulfill that dream?

2. Moses had a nice list of excuses why he wasn't able to do what God asked. What were his excuses? What excuses have you used to avoid what God has asked of you?

3. Our God is the God of Samson's strength, David's anointing, Solomon's wisdom, and Jonah's three-day stay in an underwater hotel. What name can you give Him in reference to your own life?

4. Have you ever had someone discourage you from a dream? What was your dream? Did you ever realize it?

5. Have you ever fasted for spiritual reasons? What were the results? Were they unexpected? Have you fasted since?

6. List three benefits fasting might have for your spiritual discipline.

7. "Is not this the kind of fasting I have chosen: to loose the chains of injustice and untie the cords of the yoke, to set the oppressed free and break every yoke?" (Isaiah 58:6). What do these words say to you about God's chosen fast? "I have chosen," "to loose," "untie," "set...free," and "break."

8. What is God asking you to surrender to Him? What are you afraid of? What does He promise to those who give themselves to Him?

9. Share what has happened with your party of three. How is God using you in the lives of these "three most wanted" persons? Where else is God using you? Where else would you liked to be used?

10. Share one or two of the most significant things you learned as a result of studying this book.

Roberta Kuhne conducts women's retreats and conferences throughout the United States. For more information about her availability as a speaker, write or phone:

Roberta Kuhne
8711 East Pinnacle Peak Road, No. 257
Scottsdale, AZ 85255
602/585-9582

# Notes

**CHAPTER ONE**

1. Source unknown.

2. E. C. McKenzie, *14,000 Quips & Quotes* (New York: Wings Books, 1980), 192.

**CHAPTER TWO**

1. Florence Littauer, *Personality Plus* (Old Tappan, N. J.: Fleming H. Revell Company, 1983).

2. Tim LaHaye, *Why You Act the Way You Do* (Wheaton, Ill.: Tyndale House Publishers, Inc., 1984).

3. Robert Rohm, *Positive Personality Profiles* (Atlanta: Personality Insights, Inc., 1993).

4. C. Peter Wagner, *Your Spiritual Gifts* (Ventura, Calif.: Regal Books, 1979).

5. Edward F. Murphy, *Spiritual Gifts and the Great Commission* (South Pasadena, Calif.: Mandate Press, 1975).

6. Bruce Bugbee, Don Cousins, Bill Hybels, *Network* (Fuller, Calif.: Church Growth, Fuller Institute). To order, phone 1-800-C-Fuller.

7. Wagner, *Your Spiritual Gifts,* 185.

**CHAPTER THREE**

1. Paul Quinnett, *Pavlov's Trout* (Sandpoint, Idaho: Keokee Co. Publishing, 1994) 5–7.

**CHAPTER FOUR**

1. Kurt Salierno, *To the Least of These* (Portland: Men of Letters, 1991), 11–16.

**CHAPTER SIX**

1. Story taken from a sermon by Don Doe of North Hills Community Church, Phoenix, Arizona.

2. Joseph C. Aldrich, *Gentle Persuasion* (Portland, Ore.: Multnomah Press, 1988), 60.


**CHAPTER SEVEN**

1. Frank E. Peretti, *This Present Darkness* (Wheaton, Ill.: Crossway Books, 1986), 11.


**CHAPTER EIGHT**

1. *The Zondervan Pictorial Encyclopedia of the Bible,* vol. 3 (Grand Rapids: Zondervan Corporation, 1980), 114–15.


**CHAPTER NINE**

1. Maxie D. Dunnam, *The Communicator's Commentary* (Waco, Tex.: Word, Inc., 1987), 73.

2. Arthur Wallis, *God's Chosen Fast* (Fort Washington, Pa.: Christian Literature Crusade, 1968), 41.